st nazaire 1942

the great commando raid

KEN FORD

st nazaire 1942

the great commando raid

Praeger Illustrated Military History Series

 PRAEGER

Westport, Connecticut
London

Library of Congress Cataloging-in-Publication Data

Ford, Ken, 1943–
    St Nazaire 1942: the great commando raid / Ken Ford.
       p. cm – (Praeger illustrated military history, ISSN 1547-206X)
    Originally published: Oxford: Osprey, 2001.
    Includes bibliographical references and index.
    ISBN 0-275-98280-7 (alk. paper)
    1. Saint Nazaire Raid, 1942. I. Title: Saint Nazaire, 1942. II. Series.
    D756.5.S33F67   2004
    940.54'214167–dc22   2003063220

British Library Cataloguing in Publication Data is available.

First published in paperback in 2001 by Osprey Publishing Limited, Elms Court,
Chapel Way, Botley, Oxford OX2 9LP. All rights reserved.

Library of Congress Catalog Card Number: 2003063220
ISBN: 0-275-98280-7
ISSN: 1547-206X

Praeger Publishers, 88 Post Road West, Westport, CT 06881
An imprint of Greenwood Publishing Group, Inc.
www.praeger.com

Printed in China through World Print Ltd.

The paper used in this book complies with the Permanent Paper Standard issued
by the National Information Standards Organization (Z39.48-1984).

10 9 8 7 6 5 4 3 2 1

FRONT COVER: HU2242, courtesy of the Imperial War Museum, London

ILLUSTRATED BY: Howard Gerrard

CONTENTS

KEY TO MILITARY SYMBOLS

XXXXX	XXXX	XXX	XX	X
ARMY GROUP	ARMY	CORPS	DIVISION	BRIGADE
III	II	I		
REGIMENT	BATTALION	COMPANY	INFANTRY	CAVALRY
ARTILLERY	ARMOUR	MOTORIZED	AIRBORNE	SPECIAL FORCES

THE BACKGROUND TO THE OPERATION

On 24 May 1941 the battlecruiser HMS *Hood* and the battleship HMS *Prince of Wales* confronted the German battleship *Bismarck* and the heavy cruiser *Prinz Eugen* in the north Atlantic. After just ten minutes of action the pride of the British fleet, the *Hood*, blew up and sank. The two German ships then concentrated their fire on the *Prince of Wales,* causing it some damage. The engagement was soon broken off and the British battleship withdrew, but not before *Bismarck* itself had been hit, causing her to lose fuel oil and take in sea water. Later that day she separated from the *Prinz Eugen* and set a course for the French port of St Nazaire. History will relate that she was intercepted on route by a superior British naval force and sunk.

St Nazaire contained the only dry dock on the Atlantic coast capable of handling the great German warship. The massive Normandie Dock in the port was, at that time, the largest dry dock in the world. It was completed in 1932 to hold the great passenger liner *Normandie* and remained at the centre of the important shipbuilding and repair facility that thrived in the town prior to the war. When the *Bismarck* was damaged the dockyard at St Nazaire became the immediate and obvious destination for the battleship. It was fortunate for the British that she never arrived at the port, for once safely within the heavily fortified perimeter, the ship would have posed a sustained threat to Atlantic commerce and would have been a very difficult target to attack. Indeed this point was well illustrated a little later when the two great battle

RIGHT **The town and port of St Nazaire lying on the western side of the River Loire, six miles from the sea. The Normandie Dock (Forme Ecluse Louis Joubert) is seen lying at an angle near the mid-top of the picture. At the top right, jutting out into the river, is the Old Mole. The section of water in the middle of the picture is the Submarine Basin, with the incomplete submarine pens below and the Southern Entrance to the docks on the right. (Imperial War Museum, C3465)**

cruisers *Scharnhorst* and *Gneisenau* remained holed up in Brest for several months, surviving a series of unsuccessful bombing raids by the RAF which caused them virtually no damage at all. In February 1942, they broke out of the port and dashed through the English Channel, defying the Royal Navy, the Royal Air Force and numerous coastal gun batteries to join up with other German capital ships in the relative safety of the Baltic ports.

The end of the *Bismarck* did not free the British Admiralty from the spectre of a powerful German strike force breaking loose in the Atlantic, for the *Bismarck* had an even more powerful sister ship, the *Tirpitz*, nearing completion in Germany. In 1941 Britain was fighting alone and depended on its sea routes to supply the material it needed to feed its people and to prosecute the war against the Axis powers of Germany and Italy. The success of the German submarine campaign against its shipping often caused great hardship and shortages, but the German U-boats could be attacked, and often contained, by small destroyers and frigates. Battleships and heavy cruisers were another matter entirely.

The German battleship *Bismarck* after she had been damaged by HMS *Prince of Wales* during the action in which HMS *Hood* was sunk. *Bismarck*'s fo'c'sle is lying low in the water and she is making for the great dry dock at St Nazaire on the French Atlantic coast for repair. (Imperial War Museum, HU 400)

The existence of this German battleship, the *Tirpitz*, was the prime reason for the raid. The mere threat of the ship breaking out into the north Atlantic was enough to keep several British battleships idle, waiting to react should such an event take place. (Imperial War Museum, HU2627)

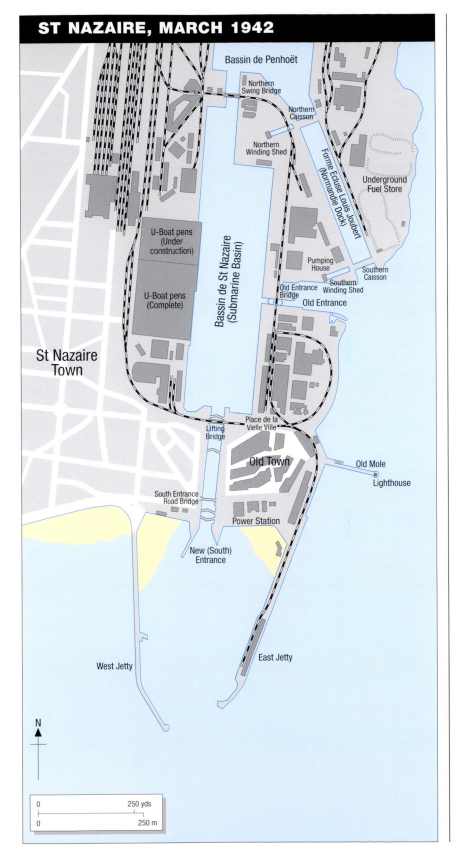

Bassin de Penhoët

Northern
Swing Bridge

Northern
Caisson

Northern
Winding Shed

Forme Écluse Louis Joubert
(Normandie Dock)

Underground
Fuel Store

U-Boat pens
(Under
construction)

U-Boat pens
(Complete)

Bassin de St Nazaire
(Submarine Basin)

Pumping
House

Southern
Caisson

Southern
Winding Shed

Old Entrance
Bridge

Old Entrance

St Nazaire
Town

Lifting
Bridge

Place de la
Vielle Ville

Old Town

Old Mole

Lighthouse

South Entrance
Road Bridge

Power Station

New (South)
Entrance

West Jetty

East Jetty

N

0   250 yds
0   250 m

These great leviathans could only be countered by other capital ships or aircraft and the availability of these weapons in the vast wastes of the North Atlantic was limited.

In January 1942 the *Tirpitz* became operational and left the Baltic for the shelter of the Norwegian fjords. The threat that the battleship posed, and the realisation of what it could do to Britain's vital supply lines, became almost an obsession with the Prime Minister, Winston Churchill. The mere existence of *Tirpitz* meant that four British capital ships had to be held in readiness at all times, waiting for her should she exit into the deep waters of the Atlantic. Added to this force were two battleships provided by the Americans, who had entered the war in December 1941. Churchill told his Chiefs of Staff that no other target was comparable to the destruction of the great German capital ship. He even went so far as to say that the whole strategy of the war turned on her mere existence. This message was not lost on the leaders of Britain's war effort who were all too aware of the *Tirpitz*'s awesome reputation. Both the Royal Navy and the Royal Air Force were already devising methods of using their hard pressed resources against the German battleship.

Whilst one arm of the Admiralty was attempting to organise the elimination of the *Tirpitz* as she lay at anchor, other planners were tackling the question of what to do should she ever break out. The Admiralty knew that if the *Tirpitz* ventured into the great Atlantic Ocean, she would need a safe refuge to return to, especially if she was unlucky enough to sustain damage such as that which befell the *Bismarck*. The only dock which was large enough to be able to take her for repairs was that provided by the port of St Nazaire. Thus, if this facility was denied to them, it was unlikely the German Navy would risk the *Tirpitz* in the Atlantic. Any aggressive sorties she might make would have to be confined to those colder waters ploughed by the Arctic convoys. A means had to be found to render the dry dock unusable.

CHRONOLOGY

1932

April, The largest dry dock in the world is completed in St Nazaire to hold the great Atlantic luxury liner *Normandie*.

1940

10 May, Hitler begins his invasion of France and the Low Countries, sweeping all opposition aside.

4 June, Bulk of the British Expeditionary Force (BEF) is evacuated from Dunkirk.

17 June, The liner *Lancastria* is sunk whilst evacuating the last troops of the BEF from St Nazaire. Over 4,500 people are missing, creating the greatest single loss of life in British maritime history.

21 June, France surrenders and signs an armistice with Germany, agreeing to the Nazi occupation of half the country. The German Army moves to occupy the whole of the Atlantic coast of France.

1941

24 May, German Battleship *Bismarck* is damaged in an action with the Royal Navy in the North Atlantic and is making for the dry dock in St Nazaire when she is sunk.

August, German battleship *Tirpitz* nears completion in the Baltic and the British Admiralty considers the possibility of her and other heavy warships being used against Allied shipping in the north Atlantic, with the dry dock at St Nazaire becoming a refuge and repair facility.

October, Admiralty considers ways of denying the Normandie Dock to the enemy, but the problem is shelved when no practicable solution can be found.

1942

January, *Tirpitz* becomes operational and leaves the Baltic for the Norwegian fjords. Churchill gives the task of eliminating the battleship the highest priority and the Chief of Combined Operations (Mountbatten) is asked to find the means of destroying the Normandie Dock.

7 February, Draft scheme for the destruction of the Normandie Dock (Operation Chariot) agreed by Mountbatten and put to Vice-Chief of Naval Staff. The plan outlines a raid by naval forces to ram the lock gates, together with a commando force to demolish port installations.

23 February, LtCol Newman appointed Military Force Commander for the raid.

25 February, Commander Ryder appointed Naval Force Commander for Operation Chariot.

3 March, Chiefs of Staff Committee finally approve the raid.

12 March, Motor Launches assemble at Falmouth.

13 March, HMS *Princess Josephine Charlotte* arrives at Falmouth with the bulk of the commandos who will take part in the operation.

18 March, MGB 314, Ryder and Newman's headquarters ship, arrives in Falmouth.

22 March, Night exercise by 'Chariot' forces test the defences of Devonport Dockyard at Plymouth. The exercise is a shambles.

25 March, HMS *Campbeltown* arrives in Falmouth with her new captain, Lt Commander Beattie, at the helm.

26 March, *Campbeltown* and the raiding flotilla of small ships sail for St Nazaire.

27 March, Force at sea.

01.34hrs, 28 March, HMS *Campbeltown* rams the outer caisson of the Normandie Dock in St Nazaire and the commandos begin their destruction of the port installations.

10.35hrs, 28 March, HMS *Campbeltown* blows up, destroying the outer lock gate and putting the Normandie Dock out of commission for the remainder of the war.

PLANNING THE RAID

The Normandie Dock at St Nazaire had, in 1942, become a strategic target of the utmost importance. It was, however, a target that proved a difficult proposition to attack. The problem of how to eliminate the dock had been challenging the planners for many months, even before Churchill had put extra pressure on his Chiefs of Staff to eliminate the threat of the *Tirpitz*. Various proposals had been put forward, but the difficulties associated with its destruction seemed insurmountable.

Precision bombing at that time was not the exact science that it became later in the war. The ability of the RAF to hit a precise target at night, in the face of concentrated enemy anti-aircraft fire was questionable. RAF raids on St Nazaire were relatively ineffective, with no vital installations ever having been knocked out. The presence of the French civilian population in close proximity to the dockyard, and a

It was known that bombing raids on port installations were not a very effective way to eliminate the vital workings of a dock. Such raids could destroy large areas of buildings and sheds, but were less likely to hit and destroy such things as lock gates, cranes and pump houses. Here high-level bombers attack the port of St Nazaire. (Imperial War Museum, C3462)

The liner *Normandie*, the pride of the French maritime fleet, in the massive dry dock in St Nazaire before the war. In the foreground is the winding shed with the long water-filled camber linking it to the outer caisson of the dock. The dock was opened by pulling the caisson on its rollers back into the camber. Immediately behind the camber is the pumping house. The dry dock also served as a lock, linking the Penhoët Basin with the River Loire. (Imperial War Museum, HL 53265)

genuine reluctance by the British government to cause innocent casualties, all meant that the RAF was unable to press home an attack that could cause damage to the dock to any significant degree. It was clear that the Normandie Dock could not be bombed out of existence, for the means of doing so were not available.

A surface raid against the heavily defended port using the techniques of the day would mean certain detection well before any landings could be made – the process of bringing a landing ship close enough to launch numbers of commando-filled landing craft to attack the docks would be sure to end in disaster. St Nazaire is located five miles up the treacherous estuary of the River Loire and is only approachable from the sea by a single narrow channel, which, in 1942, was covered by several batteries of coast defence guns. Any ship anchoring close enough to the shore to

RIGHT **The newly built luxury cruise liner *Infinity* sits in the Normandie Dock being fitted out before delivery to her owners. The view is looking towards the southern caisson, which was rammed by the *Campbeltown* during the raid. (Author's collection)**

launch small craft would be quickly blasted out of existence, as would any small landing craft that attempted the long slow run up the river to the port installations.

Special Operations Executive (SOE) was asked if it would be possible for its agents in France to sabotage the gates of the dry dock. Its planners considered the matter but concluded that the weight of explosives required and the number of covert operatives needed to carry out the task put the operation beyond its limited resources. Thus it was that the matter was put aside during 1941 as being impractical.

In January 1942 Churchill's insistence that the *Tirpitz* threat be given the highest priority resulted in the Chief of Combined Operations, Lord Louis Mountbatten, being asked to look again at finding the means of destroying the Normandie Dock. This time a new approach was found. It was known that in late March there would be exceptionally high spring tides which would allow a vessel of shallow draught free passage over the sand banks and bars that dotted the estuary of the Loire, rather than approaching the docks along the dredged, and well-protected, shipping channel. Clearly the current type of landing ship then in use by Combined Operations – converted cross-channel ferries – was unsuitable, but if a ship could be found that was both light enough to clear the shoals and heavy enough to carry a large load of explosives with which to blow the outer gate of the dry dock, then such an operation might be feasible.

With this slim chance that targeting the Normandie Dock might indeed become a possibility, Mountbatten's team at Combined Operations set to work evolving a plan. On 31 January they drafted a scheme that took account of most of the problems confronting the operation and proposed solutions to the worst of them.

It was suggested that two specially lightened destroyers would carry out the operation. The first would be packed with explosives and carry a team of commandos trained in demolition techniques. The destroyer would ram the outer gate (caisson) of the dry dock and then disembark the commandos to carry out further demolition work on the dockyard installations. The destroyer would then be blown up by delayed-action fuses, destroying the outer caisson. The second destroyer would act as an escort on the way in and then evacuate the crew of the first destroyer and the commandos once their tasks were completed. To help divert the enemy's attention whilst all this was going on, the RAF would carry out a succession of air raids in the vicinity of the port. The plan was full of imponderables and was hazardous in the extreme, but at least it formed a possible framework on which to build an operation that was of critical importance to the progress of the war.

When the plan was presented to the leaders of the Admiralty they reacted quite negatively. They could not agree to the certain loss of one of their destroyers and the distinct possibility of losing a second in the process. Even though the elimination of the Normandie Dock was a major objective of their own choosing, they stubbornly refused to provide the two obsolete destroyers that were required for the task. What they did agree to, however, was that the old Free French ship *Ouragan* could be used as the ramming ship and that a flotilla of motor launches be used to carry other commandos in and to evacuate all the men out at the end of the raid. It was not a perfect solution, but at least the plan could finally be put to the Joint Chiefs of Staff for approval.

The enthusiasm of the RAF was also waning. They did not relish the idea of being given targets not of their own choosing. The number of aircraft offered to carry out the diversionary raids by Bomber Command dwindled as the time of the operation approached, eventually falling well short of that which was required. Churchill, too, had some misgivings about the air raids fearing they might cause casualties amongst the French civilian population, and ordered that the bombing should only take place if the dockyard targets were visible.

Approval was given on 3 March and the enterprise was named Operation Chariot, but the chiefs were not happy at using a French ship, for such a move would require that French troops be used in the raid. This raised the spectre of having to deal with the leader of the Free French, General Charles de Gaulle, a difficult individual at the best of times, and would inevitably widen the circle of people who shared the secret of when and where the raid was to take place. It was felt that it would be easier to find an obsolete destroyer from within the Royal Navy, rather than accept such a compromise in security.

BUILDING AND TRAINING THE TEAM

Combined Operations was an inter-Services organisation raised with the specific role of harassing the Nazi regime. After the collapse of France, Britain stood alone against Hitler's war machine and a full-scale offensive against the enemy was beyond the resources of Britain at that time. It was unacceptable, however, for Germany to be left in unchallenged occupation of the conquered territories. Churchill was determined to cause the Germans as much alarm and confusion in those territories as possible. It was also important that the British Army did not slip into a defensive mentality, simply reacting to German moves rather than seizing the initiative itself. The offensive spirit had to be engendered and exploited both for morale at home and propaganda abroad.

The main role of Combined Operations was to carry out raids all along the enemy-occupied coastline to force the Germans to commit troops to guard important ports, coast defences and other vital installations. The mere threat that a raid might take place tied down valuable men that Hitler could use elsewhere.

Combined Operations was not a Service in its own right, but had to rely on the co-operation of the army, navy and air force to provide the support it needed for a raid. This often led to operations being modified or cancelled because the transport or resources it asked for were not made available to it. It did, however, have its own troops of army commandos with which to carry out offensive operations. These commandos, consisting of specially picked men trained in the techniques

A tug manoeuvres a submarine from 7th U-boat Flotilla in the Submarine Basin at St Nazaire. The picture was taken in the summer of 1942 after the raid. The submarine pens in the background have been completed ready to receive 6th U-boat Flotilla into the port. (Bundesarchiv, 27/1495/20)

required for raiding, were first raised just after the fall of France in 1940. In the early days things were a little disorganised and the units lacked specialised equipment and training, but as the war progressed they evolved into highly motivated teams bursting with confidence and eager for action.

By 1942 the army commandos had been organised into a Special Service Brigade of twelve individual commandos, under the overall leadership of Brigadier Charles Haydon. Each commando was about 500 strong and was made up of men from most of the corps and regiments of the army. Their training had been tough and those volunteers that survived the rigorous selection process became self-reliant, disciplined and proficient in the skills required to bring a reign of terror to the shores of Nazi-occupied Europe. Those that fell short of the mark were returned to their units.

LtCol Charles Newman was chosen to lead the commandos selected for the St Nazaire raid. Newman, a building contractor by profession, was a pre-war territorial officer from the Essex Regiment. His 38 years made him seem very old to his younger subordinates, most of whom were in their early twenties, but his skills in leadership and his ability to relate to his men, made him a popular and well-respected commanding officer. Newman had commanded 3 Independent Company in Norway in early 1940 as a major and stayed with the men of the unit as second in command when it was absorbed into 1 Special Service Battalion. The special service battalions were, however, found to be too large and unwieldy with over 1,000 officers and men and were broken down in March 1941 into individual commandos of half that size. Newman was given command of 2 Commando and spent the next year bringing it up to the peak of readiness.

With Charles Newman at the head of the commando team, it was obvious that the bulk of the men assigned to the operation would come from 2 Commando. The opportunity was also taken to give battle experience to troops from other commando units. There had been so many exercises that had been planned, rehearsed and then cancelled that there was a growing suspicion amongst the Special Service Brigade that some commandos would never see action at all. Selected men and officers from most of the other commandos were therefore assigned to Newman's task force so that someone from each of these units could be blooded in battle.

Whilst all of the soldiers earmarked for the enterprise had broad experience in raiding techniques, the St Nazaire operation required the acquisition of new skills specifically tailored to the demolition targets that awaited them. In this matter Combined Operations were lucky enough to locate an expert in dockyard demolitions. Captain Bill Pritchard was a Royal Engineer who had seen action in France in 1940 and had put his destructive skills to great use blowing bridges behind the retreating British. His father was Dock Master in Cardiff and before the war he was an engineering apprentice in the dockyards of the Great Western Railway. It was quite understandable then that his knowledge of port installations was put to good use after he arrived back from Dunkirk when he was asked to study the problem of denying dockyard facilities to the enemy. By chance, one of the docks he produced a report on, outlining the methods required to put it out of action, was St Nazaire. He concluded that machinery crucial to the dock's operation could not be effectively destroyed by random bombing. To ensure complete destruction, precise charges had to be placed at critical points on the installations themselves, and he had identified these actual sites and outlined the methods required in his report. Assisting Pritchard in the work was another sapper officer, Captain Bob Montgomery, who also had acquired a wealth of knowledge on dockyard demolition techniques. It was an extraordinary stroke of fortune for Combined Operations to locate these two officers and their combined expertise was immediately put at Newman's disposal for the raid.

Commander Robert Ryder now joined the team as commanding officer of the Royal Naval contingent of the operation. At 34 years of age he was an officer with great deal of seagoing experience: he had served three years in submarines; spent three years in command of a schooner during a long expedition to the Arctic; had the Q-ship he commanded torpedoed under him by U-boats after which he spent four days adrift at sea clinging to a wooden chock; commanded the frigate HMS *Fleetwood* for six months and lost the infantry landing ship *Prince Philippe* in a collision in thick fog. At the time of his assignment to the St Nazaire force, he was languishing in a desk job in a stately home in southern England, suffering the Admiralty's 'displeasure' at having lost his last ship. The call to join in such a marvellous enterprise as the St Nazaire raid what just the tonic he needed.

Ryder's task was to organise and implement the naval plan that would place over 200 commandos within the confines of St Nazaire dockyard to wreak havoc on its machinery, transport an ageing destroyer full of explosives right onto the southern caisson of the Normandie Dock and to withdraw all of the people involved safely back to England. It was a tall order, but he was just the man to do it, if it could be done at all.

LtCol Charles Newman's commando was to provide the fighting troops for the operation, whilst the demolition teams were to be made up from groups of officers and men from other commandos. Just over 100 of Newman's best men were selected for intensive training in the art of street

Commander Robert Edward Dudley Ryder, VC, Naval Force Commander for Operation Chariot. Prior to the raid he had been occupying a desk job at Wilton House in Wiltshire as a result of incurring the Admiralty's 'displeasure' after having lost his last ship in a collision. (Imperial War Museum, HU 1916)

The cruise liner *Infinity* now occupies the Normandie Dock, with the southern caisson to her stern in the middle of the picture. The steel lock gate offered a very small target for Beattie in Campbeltown to aim at, his task being made more difficult by enemy fire and blinding searchlights. That he found the gates at all seems to be a minor miracle of seamanship. (Author's collection)

The motor room of the pump house in the King George V Dry Dock in Southampton. The commando teams learned their demolition techniques on these giant motors and made themselves familiar with the layout of the machinery in the port. (Joe Low)

LEFT The model used during the planning and training for the raid, now on display in the Imperial War Museum, London. (Author's collection)

fighting at night, under the watchful eye of 2 Commando's second-in-command, Major Bill Copland. They were given the tasks of providing protection squads for the demolition teams, securing and holding positions crucial to the raid and with keeping the enemy at bay whilst the destruction parties went about their work.

The demolition parties were drawn from 1, 3, 4, 5, 6, 9 and 12 Commando and were sent to Burntisland on the shores of the Firth of Forth to undertake a specialised course in the destruction of dockyards. Here they were split into teams and trained by Pritchard and Montgomery in the handling of modern explosives. The role that these groups would play in the raid gradually began to evolve and each of them concentrated on the destruction of the type of target they were assigned to. The two sapper officers familiarised the men with the weight and shape of the charges they would have to place and taught them to identify the precise spot that the explosives would have to be positioned to gain maximum effect.

A naval officer and his wife pose with the officers of 2 Commando. LtCol Newman is in the centre with his pipe and stick. On the extreme left of the front row is Major Bill Copland, Newman's second in command, whilst on the extreme right of the front row is Captain D.W. Roy. (Imperial War Museum, H8204)

The troops practised over and over until they were totally confident with the explosives. They visited Rosyth dockyard to familiarise themselves with the workings of the port and to be shown the vulnerable points to be attacked: cranes, ships, locks, guns, electrical equipment and power stations were all brought to their attention and their weak points identified. Often it was not explosives that proved to be the best tool for the job, incendiaries or brute force with hammers and axes could be just as effective as a means of putting machinery and switch gear out of action.

From Burntisland the demolition teams were split into two separate groups and sent to either Cardiff or Southampton Docks in order to practice their techniques in these large commercial ports. Each of the teams were required to perform their tasks within set times, in the dark and often without key members of their group who were suddenly deemed to be casualties. Over and over they practised until they were competent enough to carry out their attack within the allotted time, blind-folded if necessary.

In Southampton they practised their demolitions on the great King George V Dry Dock, almost a replica of the Normandie Dock on which it was modelled. It was slightly longer that the French dock but less wide. Lieutenant Stuart Chant and his men perfected their task of descending the dark metal stairways of the pumping chamber to set imaginary explosives against the vulnerable impeller pumps deep below. Lieutenants Brett and Burtenshaw climbed into the hollow caisson to place charges against the steel sides, whilst Lieutenants Purdon and Smalley concentrated on blowing the winding house that provided the means of opening and closing the massive gates. After about a week, the Southampton and Cardiff groups changed over so that all of the men could get experience in all tasks, for although each party specialised in one particular demolition, if their original task was made impossible by unforeseen factors, they would be able to recognise other targets of opportunity that could be attacked

Their training was both thorough and relevant and when the time came to carry out the demolitions in France, in the dark and under intense enemy fire, the men were able to perform their tasks like clockwork.

HMS *CAMPBELTOWN* AND THE LITTLE SHIPS

By 28 March, with the planning for the raid well under way, the Admiralty had still not come up with a destroyer that could be used in the operation, but had offered a large submarine in its place. This was considered to be totally unsuitable by both Ryder and Newman. They realised that the troops would be in poor condition and vulnerable after spending three days confined in such a vessel during its long passage.

Ryder and Newman then considered using just motor launches to carry the commandos and explosives the whole way to St Nazaire and blowing the caisson by physically planting charges inside. This would be an extremely difficult proposition to put into effect and it was finally decided that it was impracticable. They resigned themselves to the fact that if no destroyer was forthcoming from the navy, then the raid would have to be cancelled. Rather than allow this to happen the Admiralty relented and offered the old destroyer *Campbeltown* to the task force to be used as the ramming ship.

HMS *Campbeltown* had started her life as the USS *Buchanan* (DD131) and was a First World War-vintage destroyer, launched in 1919. The ship had spent most of her life in reserve before being transferred to the Royal Navy, along with 50 other obsolescent American destroyers as part of the 'Lend-Lease' agreement whereby Britain allowed the Americans to 'lease' various naval bases world-wide in return for the 'loan' of badly needed ships.

HMS *Campbeltown* alongside in Devonport dockyard having arrived from the USA in September 1940. As yet unmodified for the Royal Navy, she is still showing her US Naval identity (DD131) as USS *Buchanan*. (Imperial War Museum, A952)

LEFT, TOP **Two of the Campbeltown's four funnels** were removed and blanked off, whilst the two forward stacks were modified to help give the outline of a German *Möwe* class destroyer. These funnels were shortened and cut at an angle, with the front stack enlarged to give it greater width. The picture shows the details of these modifications and two of the eight Oerlikon guns that were added to her armament. (Imperial War Museum, HU53258)

LEFT, CENTRE **Steel plating has been welded to Campbeltown's wheelhouse to give some protection from smaller calibre weapons. The forward 4in. gun has been replaced by a quicker-firing 12-pdr.** (Imperial War Museum, HU53259)

BELOW **HMS Campbeltown's fire power was boosted for the raid by the addition of eight 20mm Mark I Oerlikon guns. Four were mounted amidships, whilst four more were installed on these elevated platforms called 'band-stands'. In the foreground, work is continuing to install the long steel plates behind which the commandos would shelter during the run up to St Nazaire.** (Imperial War Museum, HU53252)

DD131 became I42 when the vessel was commissioned into the Royal Navy and became the 'Town Class' destroyer HMS *Campbeltown*. Her service with the Royal Navy was comparatively uneventful. She was assigned to the 7th Escort Group, Western Approaches, and based at Liverpool, but was almost immediately damaged in a collision which put her out of service until March 1941. For a time she was allocated to the Royal Netherlands Navy, before returning to her convoy duties under the British flag in September 1941. For the next five months she operated in the north Atlantic and had two 'kills' to her credit: she assisted in the sinking of U401 and later destroyed an enemy aircraft. On 10 March 1942 she once again appeared in Devonport for her final, and most important, refit when she was allocated to Operation Chariot and certain destruction.

To help cause some confusion to the enemy as the raiding flotilla steamed through the mouth of the Loire during the attack, *Campbeltown* was altered to resemble a German destroyer. This required a quite radical transformation which included removing two of her four stacks and then cutting the tops of the other two at an angle to resemble the German class of ship. The forward funnel was then enlarged to almost twice the original width and the second funnel was shortened somewhat, helping to imitate the distinctive outline of the *Möwe* class of destroyer. To help safeguard the crew and the troops on board, extra metal plating and splinter mats were added to the bridge and two parallel rows of armoured-plate panels were welded to the decks in order to give some protection for the commandos as they lay in the open during *Cambeltown*'s final run into the port.

Whilst it was passing through the German coast defences on its passage up the Loire, *Campbeltown* needed lots of rapid fire power to help counter the enemy guns. The forward 4in. gun was removed and replaced with a 12-pdr and eight 20mm Mark 1 Oerlikon cannons were added, mounted on elevated platforms.

The destroyer was stripped of all items not essential to the raid in order to make it as light as possible: all heavy gear was removed, torpedo tubes cut away, magazines emptied and every redundant item in the ship landed. When she finally set sail for St Nazaire with just the amount of fuel and water that she would require for the one-way journey, *Campbeltown* drew just 11 feet of water. There had been, however, one vital addition to her cargo for this voyage, for inside her forward compartments lay four and a quarter tons of explosives.

The problem of organising this explosive punch was given to a 28-year-old Royal Navy officer, Lt Nigel Tibbits. He decided to use 24 Mark VII depth charges, each weighing 400lbs. The charges were grouped together in a special steel tank which was then covered in concrete. Three long-delay pencil fuses were inserted in the charge and linked together with cordtex (instantaneous detonating fuse). The explosives were primed to explode after a predicted eight-hour delay, giving ample time for the crew of the *Campbeltown* and the commandos to do their work and make their escape.

Lt Commander Stephen Halden Beattie, VC, captain of the *Campbeltown* during the raid. Beattie was a contemporary of Commander Ryder, the men having been shipmates during their days as cadets. (Imperial War Museum, HU1917)

The 'little ships'

The 'little ships' which made up the remainder of the raiding force were of three types. The majority were Fairmile 'B' motor launches, some armed with cannon and some carrying torpedoes. In addition to these there was a heavily armed motor gun boat and a specially converted motor torpedo boat.

The Fairmile 'B' motor launch was the most common type of motor launch built in Britain during the war. They were employed by various coastal forces flotillas in an anti-submarine, escort or patrol role. The launches were Admiralty-designed to be constructed in a prefabricated form and assembled at various yards throughout the country. By 1945 over 560 of them had been built in more than 70 individual shipyards and they were in service all over the world with the Royal Navy as well as various other Commonwealth navies. The Fairmile 'B' was of wooden

Fairmile 'B' Class launch, the most numerous of the small vessels used in the raid. This illustration shows the type of motor launch, but not one that actually took part in the St Nazaire operation. Its forward armament is a 3-pdr Hotchkiss, whilst aft is a 20mm Oerlikon. On the bridge are two twin Lewis .303in. machine-guns. (Imperial War Museum, A13625)

construction, 112ft long, 19½ft across the beam, powered by two 600 horsepower Hall-Scott petrol engines, giving a maximum top speed of 20 knots.

For the St Nazaire raid, 28 Motor Launch Flotilla, commanded by Lt Commander F.N. Wood, provided eight Fairmiles, whilst a further four came from Lt Commander W.L. Stephens's 20 Motor Launch Flotilla. All of these craft eventually had their weapons modified in order to give more firepower – the single Hotchkiss 3-pdr gun mounted forward was replaced by two Oerlikon 20mm guns mounted fore and aft. On the bridge were two .303in. Lewis machine-guns. Just before the raid these 12 craft were augmented by the arrival of four more Fairmile 'B's from 7 Motor Launch Flotilla. They were provided to give an offensive capability should the raiding convoy run into any enemy ships, for the craft were all motor torpedo boats armed with two 18in. torpedo tubes, one mounted each side of the funnel. Their late arrival meant that there was not enough time to install new Oerlikons, so they kept their single 3-pdr guns.

The one motor gun boat allocated to the raiders was MGB 314. This craft came from 14 Motor Gun Boat Flotilla and was a Fairmile 'C' class launch. Like the other classes of Fairmiles, the 'C' class was prefabricated and assembled in various shipyards. Between June and August 1941 24 were built. Slightly smaller than the 'B' class, MGB 314 was powered by three 850 horsepower Hall-Scott engines able to give her a top speed of 26 knots. She was well armed for a craft of her size with two 2-pdr guns mounted fore and aft and two power-operated twin 0.5in. heavy machine-guns mounted amidships. MGB 314 was also equipped with radar and an echo-sounder and was therefore selected as headquarters ship for the raid. Her sounding equipment would be most useful when crossing the shoals in the Loire estuary. She was therefore designated lead craft for the raid – both Ryder and Newman were on board as she made the run up the river to St Nazaire. The extra armament, equipment and engines did, however, limit her seagoing range considerably and even with extra fuel tanks added she still had to be towed very close to the target in order to conserve fuel for the return journey.

MGB 314 was from 14 Motor Gun Boat Flotilla and was a Fairmile 'C' Class launch. Her three Hall-Scott engines gave her a maximum speed of 26 knots. She was quite strongly armed for a small craft, with a very exposed hand-operated Vickers 2-pdr pom-pom forward (the position from which Able Seaman Savage won his VC), amidships were two twin power-operated 0.5in. machine-guns, and aft was another 2-pdr, a Rolls semi-automatic. MGB 314 was used as headquarters vessel for Newman and Ryder during the run up the Loire. (Imperial War Museum, HU53260)

The final type of craft in the small flotilla was MTB 74, commanded by SubLt R. Wynn. She was a specially modified 70ft motor torpedo boat built by Vospers in 1940. Her modifications consisted of mounting her two torpedo tubes on the foredeck instead of amidships. These alterations were completed with a specific task in mind. The German battlecruiser *Scharnhorst* in Brest harbour seemed beyond reach of the attentions of the Royal Navy, but a suggestion was made that a fast craft carrying modified torpedoes – long tubes of explosives with no propulsion unit— might get close enough to the *Scharnhorst* to shoot the missiles over the anti-torpedo net that surrounded the ship, sink to the bottom and then explode after a suitable time delay. Clearly such a mission would be suicidal for the crew of the MTB, but the plans went ahead nonetheless, only to be dropped when the battlecruiser, together with the *Gneisenau* and *Prinz Eugen*, broke out of Brest and made for the Baltic. With the *Scharnhorst* raid no longer practicable, MTB 74 was left looking for a suitable job at the time when the St Nazaire raid was being considered. Early in the planning stages it was proposed that she might be used to torpedo the inner caisson of the Normandy Dock, or one of the lock gates into the Submarine Basin.

MTB 74 was over 40ft shorter that the other motor launches, but still mounted five engines: three 1,250 supercharged Packard and two Ford V8s. The Packards gave her a top speed of almost 40 knots, whilst the Fords provided power for slow-speed manoeuvring. This combination did mean that she could either surge ahead at 35 knots or crawl along at six, but was incapable of the even 15 knots of the remainder of the raiding force. MTB 74 was therefore towed most of the way to St Nazaire.

This collection of small ships, all modified especially for the raid, were engaged to complete a task for which they were not built. They

MTB 74 alongside in Portsmouth Harbour after its special modifications for the proposed attack on the battle-cruiser *Scharnhorst* at Brest. The operation did not take place because the German warship, along with the *Gneisenau* and *Prinz Eugen*, broke out of the port and made their way back to Germany. (Vosper Thornycroft)

were seaworthy enough to make the journey and to carry the commandos right up to their objectives, but they lacked the strength to take any punishment from the enemy. They were being asked to sail under scores of German guns all of which were of larger calibre than anything the motor launches carried. Apart from some thin armour round the bridge and the provision of splinter mats, they had nothing but their wooden sides with which to protect their crew and passengers. Their hulls were so thin that even a rifle bullet could penetrate their frail sides. Their vulnerability was further increased when all of the craft had deck-mounted tanks of highly flammable petrol installed to increase the range necessary to make the voyage to St Nazaire and back.

THE ENEMY

In March 1942 France was a divided nation. The Germans had taken over the northern part and the Atlantic coast which they had seized during their blitzkrieg drive through Europe in 1940, whilst the southern half of the country was governed by a puppet French government in Vichy, led by Marshal Petain.

The Nazi regime swiftly began adapting France's industrial power to its own military needs. The great Atlantic seaports became bases from which to wage undersea war against Great Britain and her allies. By the end of December 1941, the Germans had established U-boat bases in Brest, Lorient, St Nazaire, La Rochelle and Bordeaux (for Italian U-boats). These bases now became vital for the pursuit of the war and they were converted into fortresses to forestall any seaborne assault against them. To protect the submarines from air attack whilst being re-supplied or refitted, huge concrete pens were built. These were massive structures, able to withstand the heaviest of aerial bombing and taking years to complete. The one in St Nazaire was only two-thirds built at the time of the raid.

Around St Nazaire, at the entrance to the River Loire, the existing obsolete 194mm coast defences installed by the French in their 5th Naval District, were improved by the addition of fixed emplacements containing weapons of various calibre. The crews of these guns were all German naval troops under the command of Kapitän zur See Zuckschwerdt. He was designated See Kommandant Loire and was

Two of the four gun emplacements that housed the 170mm guns of Dieckmann's 280th Naval Artillery Battalion on the headland at Pointe de l'Eve. The whole site together with its magazines, command post, troop shelters and fire control post is in remarkably good condition. (Author's collection)

responsible for the seaward defences around the estuary and for the anti-aircraft defences of the port. His headquarters was in La Baule, a seaside resort eight miles to the west of St Nazaire. Zuckschwerdt's command consisted of a battalion of coast defence guns, a brigade of anti-aircraft artillery (much of which was able to be used in a dual role against naval targets) and the various local defence forces of the Harbour Commander St Nazaire.

The coastal artillery was manned by 280th Naval Artillery Battalion under the command of Kapitän zur See Edo Dieckmann, who had his headquarters at Chémoulin Point. Dieckmann's battalion contained 28 guns of calibre from 75mm to the great 240mm railway guns at La Baule. These were the long-range guns sited to engage hostile ships well before they entered the mouth of the Loire.

The lighter guns, which had a dual role as anti-aircraft and coast defence weapons, were manned by 22nd Naval Flak Brigade, commanded by Kapitän zur See Karl-Conrad Mecke from his headquarters in the village of St Marc. He had three battalions of naval gunners at his disposal: 703rd Naval Flak Battalion commanded by Korvettenkapitän Thiessen; 705th Naval Flak Battalion commanded by Korvettenkapitän Koch and 809th Naval Flak Battalion under the command of Korvettenkapitän Burhenne. These three units comprised 43 guns between them, mostly of 20mm and 40mm calibre, with a few 37mm cannons among them, covering the closer waters of the estuary and the port of St Nazaire itself. They were also responsible for the defence of the area against air attack. Also part of Mecke's command were the searchlights which lit the river and illuminated targets for the guns. Four large 150mm searchlights covered the estuary of the Loire, whilst numerous 60mm lights provided the back-up for the lighter quick-firing guns closer to the port.

Within the port itself the Harbour Commander Korvettenkapitän Kellermann looked after the close defence of the dockyard with his guard companies, armed with light weapons and machine-guns. Kellermann also controlled the harbour defence boats which patrolled the river and the mouth of the Loire.

Also immediately concerned with dockyard defence were the men who were employed within the port itself. These comprised naval technicians (organised into 2 and 4 Works Companies), workers from Organisation Todt, crews of the ships in harbour, U-boat maintenance groups (though not the U-boat crews) and various other miscellaneous German workers. All of these men were capable of bearing arms and all of them could pose a threat to the raiding force. On the night that the commandos carried out the raid, there were four harbour defence boats and ten ships from 16 and 42 Minesweeper Flotillas in the basins, as well as two German tankers in the Normandie Dock itself.

Altogether, this put around 5,000 German personnel in and around St Nazaire when the little ships of Operation Chariot carrying their 600 men sailed quietly into the mouth of the Loire. Further afield, to the west along the coast in La Baule, was the corps headquarters of General Ritter von Prager. His 333rd Infantry Division covered this sector of the coast. The division had been formed in January 1941 and was largely made up of Polish troops. It was to have a relatively short life, for early in 1943 the division was transferred to the southern sector of the Eastern

Front. Within six months it had been so badly mauled that it had ceased
to exists as a fighting unit and was disbanded.

The division had arrived in Brittany earlier that year and was given
the task of covering the coastline from St Nazaire to Lorient. One of its
regiments, 679th Infantry Regiment, was headquartered just west of La
Baule and had its troops stationed in various villages inland from the
port, ready to move against the coast should a British landing take place.
The division was a long-term garrison for the area and not placed on
immediate alert, so when the commandos attacked it took some time to
mobilise its units against the raiders.

Although the Normandie Dock was undoubtedly a great asset to
them, most Germans around St Nazaire saw the U-boat pens as the most
vital objective within the port. The great concrete facility provided a
safe anchorage for the boats of 7th Submarine Flotilla and part of
6th Submarine Flotilla, which was gradually being transferred to
St Nazaire. With Hermann Göring's Luftwaffe heavily engaged in the
war against Russia, the German U-boat arm was the only tool with which
the Third Reich could wage war directly against Britain at that time. The
defences of the port were planned in expectation of landings aimed at
knocking out the U-boat facility and were thought to be more than
adequate to repel any invader. Indeed, the day before the commandos
stormed ashore, Admiral Dönitz, Flag Officer U-boats, visited St Nazaire
and asked Kapitänleutnant Herbert Sohler, commander 7th Submarine
Flotilla, what he would do if the British landed in the port. 'It would be
out of the question for the English to enter the harbour,' replied Sohler.
At that moment, not too far away in the Bay of Biscay, LtCol Newman,
Captain Ryder and their men were heading his way and were about to
make him eat his words.

THE FINAL PLAN

With the selection of the armada of vessels that would carry the raiding force to its target made, the modifications carried out and the training of the commandos complete, it was time to bring the whole force together. In mid-March all the participating parties and their craft began to assemble at Falmouth, the port of embarkation for the operation.

The arrival of such numbers of motor launches all supplemented with extra fuel tanks and unusual armament required a plausible cover story to allay idle talk around the town and amongst the other service personnel stationed there. It was decided to create a story that the craft were being organised into 10th Anti-submarine Striking Force, whose role was long-range anti-submarine sweeps in the Bay of Biscay.

The commando protection parties from 2 Commando arrived from Scotland aboard the landing ship *Princess Josephine Charlotte*, a converted Belgian North Sea ferry. They were to remain on board, mainly out of sight, until the raiding force left for St Nazaire. The demolition parties assembled straight from their exploits in the docks of Cardiff and Southampton.

The commandos were now introduced to the small ships and given a chance to find their sea legs. The troops were taken on a long sea trip around the Scilly Isles in rough weather. The craft pitched and rolled in the heavy sea and virtually every man aboard was sick. Training and familiarisation continued throughout the two weeks the force was assembled, with the motor launches practising coming alongside jetties in the dark, keeping station in open seas and finally carrying out a night assault on the dockyard of Plymouth – the attack force was easily detected by the port's defences and the exercise ended in a shambles, one particular problem being that the ships' crews were largely blinded by the defences' searchlights.

On 23 March HMS *Atherstone* and *Tynedale* arrived in Falmouth. These two 'Hunt' class destroyers were to act as escort ships to the raiding flotilla, helping to protect the extremely vulnerable group on their journey to the mouth of the Loire. And late on the afternoon of 25 March, *Campbeltown* arrived to join the party. She looked extremely odd with her shortened and raked funnels and caused a stir amongst the older hands as they saw her very Germanic outline silhouetted against the low sun. She had a new master, as the previous captain was considered too old for the raid and replaced by Lt Commander Stephen Beattie. Ryder was pleased with this change as Beattie and he were old friends, having both been together as cadets in the training ship HMS *Thunderer*.

By this time assembly of the raiding force was complete and it was now time to brief all the parties involved as to the target and purpose of the operation. As each man learned of his role and of the overwhelming

HMS *Princess Josephine Charlotte*, a converted Belgian cross-Channel ferry used by the commandos as a landing ship. It was also an accommodation vessel for the troops whilst in Falmouth harbour. (Imperial War Museum, A9756)

odds that the raiding party would have to face, it became quite clear that many of them would, in all probability, not return. An opportunity was given for any who wished to remain behind to do so, without any recriminations or loss of honour, but none came forward to drop out. For better or worse, they were all in this together.

The objectives of the raid were now made clear. They were ranged in order of priority: first, the destruction of the two caissons of the Normandie Dock; second, the demolition of dockyard facilities supporting the dry dock such as the winding sheds and the pumping house; third, the wrecking of all lock gates to render the internal basins tidal and, finally, to attack any shipping, especially U-boats, that could be attacked as targets of opportunity.

To complete these tasks, the raiding force was organised as follows: the main charge to blow out the southern caisson of the Normandie Dock would be carried right up to the gate by HMS *Campbeltown*; demolition and protection parties of commandos would then land from the ship and set about destroying the local defences, the pump house, the northern caisson and the two winding sheds; other commando demolition parties, carried to St Nazaire in the motor launches, would land at the Old Mole and Old Entrance and attack local defences, bridges, locks and equipment, eventually sealing off the area around the Old Mole to enable an orderly re-embarkation. In addition, the motor torpedo boat MTB 74 would torpedo the outer lock at the northern entrance of the Submarine Basin and help render the basin tidal.

The passage to St Nazaire was to be made in company with two protecting destroyers, *Atherstone* and *Tynedale*, with the motor launches and destroyers adopting a sub-hunting formation as a cover should the small fleet be spotted by enemy aircraft. Nearer the entrance to the River Loire, the escorting destroyers would leave the flotilla and the raiding force would adopt battle formation. MGB 314, with its radar and echo sounder, would be in the lead guiding the force across the mud flats and shallows. On either side of the gun boat would be two motor torpedo boats, ML 160 and ML 270. These were to act as lead protection, able to fire their torpedoes at any vessel interfering with the force. Next would come the *Campbeltown* with two columns of motor

The last aerial reconnaissance picture taken immediately before the raid, showing German ships in harbour and two tankers in the Normandie Dock. The photograph shows the dock to be dry and the outer caisson at the southern end closed, a combination that was necessary to allow the gate to be rammed by *Campbeltown*. (Imperial War Museum, C2594)

launches on either side and to its rear; the port column destined to land its troops on the Old Mole, whilst the starboard column aimed to put its men down alongside the Old Entrance. Bringing up the rear would be two more MTBs, ML 446 and ML 298, providing rear protection. Finally, MTB 74, with its erratic momentum, would try to keep station as it waited for its opportunity to torpedo the lock in the Old Entrance.

After landing their troops, the launches were to wait in the river until the demolition tasks were completed. Re-embarkation of the commandos was to take place from the Old Mole. The crew of the *Campbeltown* were to be picked up from around the Old Entrance once the destroyer had been evacuated. The four torpedo-carrying motor launches which acted as front and rear protection, MLs 160, 170, 298 and 446, were to carry no passengers to St Nazaire, but would provide the capacity for embarking troops and crew after the raid.

The operation was due to take place on the night of 28/29 March, the night of the highest tides in the Loire, but Ryder felt that the assembled force was ready for action and, afraid of losing the prevailing good weather, decided to bring the assault forward by a day. In consequence, on the afternoon of 26 March, the small fleet slipped anchor and made out of Falmouth and into the Channel bound for France.

THE SEA JOURNEY

The voyage to St Nazaire took the flotilla across the mouth of the English Channel, round the Brittany peninsula and through the Bay of Biscay. Once the raiding force had left the sheltered and heavily patrolled home waters, then it ran the risk of being spotted by German aircraft, U-boats or surface vessels. Even if not engaged by these interceptors, its course and position would be reported and monitored by the enemy. It was necessary, therefore, to mislead the Germans as to its destination and purpose.

Once clear of British waters it assumed the formation of an anti-submarine sweep. From the air the three destroyers and eighteen motor launches looked very convincing in the part. The course set for St Nazaire took the fleet clear of the French coast, well out to sea. If the flotilla was spotted and tracked by the enemy, then it was hoped they would assume they were heading for Gibraltar. Even when the vessels finally turned towards the French coast, they would do so well past the mouth of the River Loire seemingly aiming for La Rochelle. Finally, they would approach the estuary from the south, thus concealing their ultimate destination until the last few hours.

The convoy made a steady ten knots as it ploughed south-westerly, with *Atherstone* in the lead, flanked by *Tynedale*, towing MGB 314, and *Campbeltown*, towing MTB 74. Strung out on either bow came the long lines of motor launches. Six hours into the voyage, the last of the lone hurricane fighters that had been shepherding the convoy swept low

The destroyer HMS *Tynedale* was assigned to the operation along with HMS *Atherstone* as protection vessels during the voyage to St Nazaire. The two ships then waited during the night 25 miles offshore, to shepherd home those vessels that survived the raid. (Imperial War Museum, FL22770)

down the columns of ships and headed north for home. At 19.00hrs the raiders swung to the south, in order to give the minefield off Ushant a wide berth.

The night passage was uneventful and the dawn of 27 March brought a cloudless sky and light winds. Visibility was excellent, much to the annoyance of Commander Ryder, who would rather have had heavy cloud and mist with which to screen his force. At 07.00hrs the fleet was 160 miles to the south-west of St Nazaire and changed course slightly to the east to start its long turn towards the French coast. Speed was reduced to eight knots. A few minutes later, *Tynedale* sighted an object on the surface seven miles away to the east and altered course to investigate, after first having cast off MGB 314.

It quickly became clear that the object was a German U-boat on the surface and the *Tynedale* increased speed to intercept. The submarine was stationary and spotted the destroyer at about five miles. It fired off a rocket as a recognition signal and *Tynedale* replied with five white flashes of her lamp. This was pure guesswork by her commander, but the German captain seemed to be satisfied with the reply. At 5,000 yards the destroyer opened fire, scoring several near misses. The U-boat crash dived and made to escape. Thirteen minutes later the *Tynedale* dropped a pattern of depth charges across the area. The shock of the explosions caused the submarine to break surface and to dive again almost immediately. *Tynedale* opened fire again at close range and straddled the submarine just before she disappeared. The destroyer then began a search of the area, trying to locate the enemy with ASDIC.

Atherstone now came up to join in the sweep and for the next two hours the destroyers hunted for the U-boat. Nothing more was heard and eventually Ryder decided to break off the search hoping that the submarine had been sunk. The destroyers set off at high speed to join *Campbeltown* and the rest of the flotilla. Ryder was worried that the submarine had seen the raiding force and had managed to get off a siting report. For the next few hours all eyes scanned the sky to see if enemy reconnaissance aircraft were sent to follow up any report.

Ryder was in luck for the U-boat encountered was the U-593, which had been returning to St Nazaire from its very first patrol. She had spotted the raiding force, but had not reported the sighting before she crash dived. It was not until her commander, Kapitänleutnant Gerd Kelbling, felt safe enough to surface at 14.20hrs that he got off a report to German Group Command West, signalling that he had seen three destroyers and 10 MTBs heading west. The make-up of the group and the mistake in reporting the actual course (the force was heading south-east) led the enemy to believe that it was a mine-laying operation, or a group of craft on passage to Gibraltar.

Not long after the encounter with U-593, the flotilla ran into a fleet of French fishing boats. It was believed that the Germans often put observers aboard these vessels with radios to report on any British movements. Ryder had previously decided to sink any such boats should his force run across them. However, the number of trawlers in this fleet made it logistically impossible to sink them all so he sent *Atherstone* and *Tynedale* to investigate, choosing to sink just two of the boats after having taken off their crews. The Frenchmen assured Ryder that no German observers or radio sets were carried on board any of the craft.

As the day wore on, the sky became overcast and the clouds descended to give some cover to the raiding force. In the late morning alarming news was received from Plymouth that five German destroyers had been observed on the latest reconnaissance photographs taken of St Nazaire docks and might be met in the vicinity of the port. In the event, the destroyers had put to sea before Ryder's force arrived and were patrolling the submarine lanes off St Nazaire in response to U-593's signal that the force he had spotted might be laying mines.

At 18.30hrs one of the motor launches, ML 341, commanded by Lt D. Briault, had the misfortune to lose its port engine to a mechanical failure. Such an unfortunate incident had been foreseen in the planning stage and Lt Falconar now brought his near-empty ML 446 up from the rear of the line to take ML 341's party of commandos on board. The transfer took some time to complete and it took a further two hours before Falconar caught up with the rest of the flotilla, joining the rear of the column just as they reached the Loire estuary. Unable to fix the engine with sufficient speed to make up the lost time, Briault was forced to return to England alone.

The force made a steady eight knots and pressed on closer to the French coast. Two more changes of course brought the little ships in line with St Nazaire and at 20.00hrs they began to close directly on the port. It was here that the escorting destroyers *Atherstone* and *Tynedale* took their leave of the group. MGB 314 was cast off from *Atherstone* and Commander Ryder and LtCol Newman left the destroyer to go aboard what was now to become their headquarters ship. Parting signals were flashed between the vessels as the two destroyers slipped away to set up a standing patrol off the Loire and wait for the return of the raiding force.

Lt Curtis at the helm of MGB 314 now brought his craft to the head of the line and the raiding force assumed battle formation for the run into the port. Speed was increased to 12 knots. There was, however, one

The Submarine HMS *Sturgeon* lay in wait off the mouth of the River Loire in order to provide a very precise navigational beacon for the raiders. (Imperial War Museum, A14360)

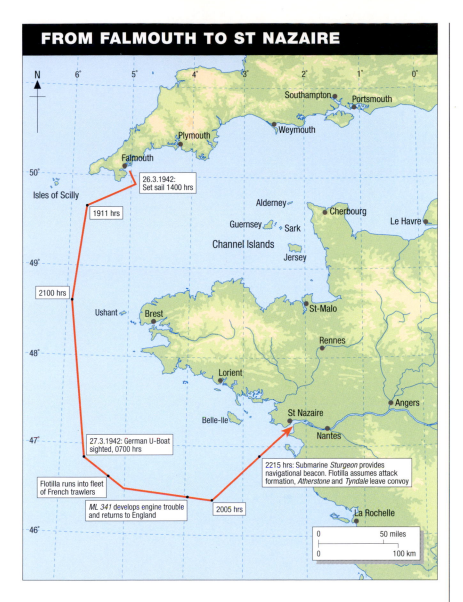

FROM FALMOUTH TO ST NAZAIRE

26.3.1942:
Set sail 1400 hrs

1911 hrs

2100 hrs

27.3.1942: German U-Boat
sighted, 0700 hrs

Flotilla runs into fleet
of French trawlers

ML 341 develops engine trouble
and returns to England

2005 hrs

2215 hrs: Submarine *Sturgeon* provides
navigational beacon. Flotilla assumes attack
formation, *Atherstone* and *Tyndale* leave convoy

Southampton · Portsmouth · Weymouth · Plymouth · Falmouth · Isles of Scilly · Alderney · Cherbourg · Le Havre · Guernsey · Sark · Channel Islands · Jersey · St-Malo · Ushant · Brest · Rennes · Lorient · Angers · Belle-Ile · St Nazaire · Nantes · La Rochelle

last rendezvous to be made before Ryder's force was set loose against the enemy. It was vitally important that the final run up the Loire was made along a very specific and narrow course, which would take it over the mud flats and shoals at a most precise point. To aid the flotilla, the British submarine *Sturgeon*, commanded by Lt Commander Mervyn Wingfield, was to be waiting at Point Z, acting as a navigational beacon from which the force could get a pin-point chart position.

At 22.00hrs, *Sturgeon*'s light was spotted dead ahead. Operation Chariot was exactly on time and on position – the final run into the jaws of death could now begin.

THE RUN UP
THE RIVER LOIRE

At about midnight the Royal Air Force raid on the port began, but without a great deal of success. The plan called for the bombing of the docks to continue until the ships began their run up the river and then to switch to the town, whilst the docks were attacked by the Operation Chariot force. The overcast sky and low cloud that night meant that the bombing could not be pressed home for fear of causing French casualties. All the RAF could do was to circle around the area hoping to keep the enemy's attention drawn skywards.

In *Campbeltown*, Lt Tibbets had set and activated the pencil fuses deep in the forward compartments of the warship. Come what may, eight hours later the huge charge would explode when the acid had eaten through the copper restraining wire and operated the detonators. This time delay was not, however, absolutely accurate and there was a margin of error involved, but in any case the charge would not go up before 05.00hrs at the earliest and by 09.00hrs at the latest, easily enough time for the raiders to complete their destructive tasks and withdraw.

As the bombers droned overhead, the Charioteers closed inexorably on the port. Tension began to mount as each man, especially the commanders, waited for the Germans to discover the force. The radar station at Le Croisic was passed without raising any alarm. The fleet pressed on through the dark waters towards the estuary of the River Loire. All remained quiet, with no searchlights probing the sea; everyone held their breath.

At 00.30hrs, the convoy entered the wide mouth of the river when it passed the ghostly wreck of the liner *Lancastria*, sunk in 1940, the scene of the greatest loss of life in British maritime history. Fifteen minutes later, the raiders passed by the Banc de Chatelier right opposite the 75mm guns on the Pointe de Gildas. Still unobserved, the force continued on its course towards the port. Ahead the bombing was becoming sporadic, with often just a single aircraft circling around.

On shore, Kapitän zur See Mecke was starting to become suspicious. The air raid was not developing as it should. Instead of squadrons of aircraft releasing tons of explosives on the port and then making for home, individual aircraft were circling around dropping the odd missile seemingly at random. Mecke thought that there was 'some devilry afoot' and sent a signal to all his units to be on their guard. At 24.00hrs he warned that: 'The conduct of the enemy aircraft is inexplicable and indicates suspicion of parachute landings.' At 01.00hrs he ordered his guns to cease fire in order not to assist the bombers in finding the location of the port. He also ordered the searchlights to be extinguished. He further urged his men to maintain a 'continued and increased alert' and for them to direct special attention seaward.

Kapitän zur See Karl-Conrad Mecke, commander of 22nd Naval Flak Brigade, after he had been presented with the Knight's Cross by Grand Admiral Dönitz. It was Mecke who, suspicious of the erratic behaviour of the RAF aircraft during their diversionary raid on St Nazaire, alerted his coast defences that some 'devilry' was afoot. (Bundesarchiv, 74/142/2)

Two enemy sailors display a German flag to the camera as a trophy from the raid. This picture dated the day of the attack creates something of a puzzle. The German flag flown by *Campbeltown* was supposed to have been cut up as souvenirs immediately it was hauled down, during the run into the port. Was *Campbeltown* flying two German flags? (Bundesarchiv, 65/2314/19A)

At about this time the raiders slipped quietly past the next shoal, Les Jardinets, coming ever closer to the north shore of the Loire. They were now just over two miles from Chémoulin Point and Edo Dieckmann's 150mm guns and still they remained unobserved by the enemy. From here on in the little fleet began passing over the mud flats and sand banks. The normal dredged shipping channel, Charpentiers Channel, swung northwards at this point to passed right under the German guns close to the shore. *Campbeltown* and her fleet of little ships made a straight line for the docks over the shallows that riddled the mouth of the Loire. Twice she touched bottom, but her momentum carried her forward without altering her engine revolutions.

At 01.20hrs they slipped by Les Morées Tower, but seconds later the piercing beam of a searchlight blazed into life and swept the sea behind them. Then, just as suddenly, it went out. They were now just under two miles from the target, still apparently undetected and closing on the docks. It all seemed to be too good to be true, and it was. The force had been spotted as early as 01.15hrs, when a lookout at St Marc reported the approach of a force of about 17 vessels. He reported this to the Harbour Commander's headquarters, but the sighting was dismissed out of hand; they were not expecting any ships and so refused to believe that any were approaching. The sighting was passed on to Mecke's headquarters and the staff there also contacted the Harbour Master's HQ and received the same reply. Mecke was then told of the sighting and he reacted quite differently. At 01.20hrs he signalled to all units in the St Nazaire area the message: 'Beware landing.' This set in motion a

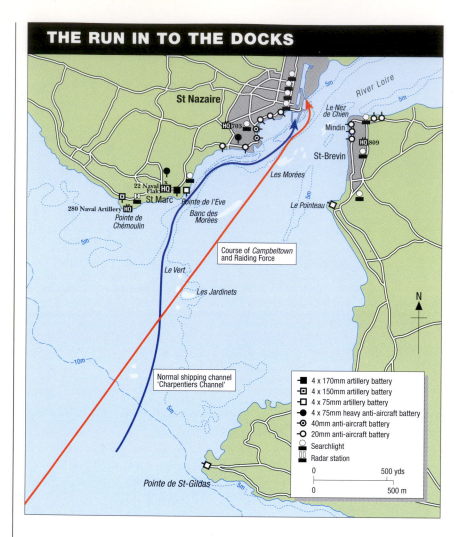

THE RUN IN TO THE DOCKS

St Nazaire

River Loire

Le Nez de Chien

Mindin

HQ 703

HQ 809

St-Brevin

Les Morées

22 Naval Flak

HQ

St Marc

Pointe de l'Eve

280 Naval Artillery HQ

Pointe de Chémoulin

Banc des Morées

Le Pointeau

Course of *Campbeltown* and Raiding Force

Le Vert

Les Jardinets

N

Normal shipping channel 'Charpentiers Channel'

■ 4 x 170mm artillery battery
▣ 4 x 150mm artillery battery
□ 4 x 75mm artillery battery
● 4 x 75mm heavy anti-aircraft battery
◉ 40mm anti-aircraft battery
◎ 20mm anti-aircraft battery
▮ Searchlight
▥ Radar station

| 0 | 500 yds |
| 0 | 500 m |

Pointe de St-Gildas

great train of events as throughout all commands emergency orders designed to prevent a landing were put into effect. All available troops, ships' crews, harbour defence vessels, shore defenders and rear area personnel were summoned to counter enemy landings.

All the searchlights, on both banks of the river, now came to life and began probing the dark water, quickly locking onto the grey destroyer and her fleet of little ships. At first sight *Campbeltown* resembled one of the huge Möwe-class destroyers with the German flag fluttering at her mast. But something was wrong, the ships had come out of the night, totally unexpectedly. With no one willing to make a fool of himself, there was some hesitation as to what to do next. Some gun crews fired a few rounds of light cannon fire low over the flotilla. The ships were then challenged by German signal stations on each bank. Leading Signalman Pike on board the *Campbeltown* had been prepared for this and began replying to the challenge, flashing out his message in German. 'Wait,' he signalled. Then gave the call sign of a torpedo-boat known to the raiders. Without waiting for the enemy to follow up on this, Pike flashed a signal prefixed 'Urgent', which gave the message: 'Two craft damaged by enemy action, request permission to proceed to harbour without delay.' The Germans stopped firing.

After a short delay the Germans started firing again, this time from heavier guns on the north bank, Dieckmann's batteries at Chémoulin Point and Point de l'Eve. Pike started signalling again: 'You are firing on friendly ships.' Again the firing stopped. The *Campbeltown* was now just six minutes from target, entering the River Loire proper and gradually leaving behind the heavier guns on the north shore.

The Germans were now certain that the ships were hostile and Mecke and Dieckmann ordered every battery and gun emplacement to open fire on them. The bluff had worked better than anyone could have imagined – the fleet had nearly reached the target. But the game was up. Ryder ordered all of his vessels to return fire. *Campbeltown* was the first to respond, her crew ran down the German flag and hoisted the White Ensign then opened up with their rapid-firing Oerlikons, the little ships did likewise. In an instant the whole river erupted into a gigantic fireworks display as multicoloured tracer criss-crossed over the surface of the river, striking the flotilla of ships and ricocheting off anything it caught with a glancing blow. Return fire from the massed guns of the coast defences crashed amongst the spread-out vessels which immediately began to take hits and suffer casualties.

With five minutes to go to the target it was a case of letting rip with everything and making for the docks with all speed. At the head of the convoy, MGB 314 reached the outer harbour and pressed on past a guard ship, or *Sperrbrecher*, moored just off the East jetty. The German ship had joined in the barrage and was pouring a great volume of fire into the British flotilla steaming towards it. At very close range all of MGB 314's weapons turned on the enemy ship, riddling its decks with explosive shells. The *Sperrbrecher* fell silent amid screams of agony from her wounded crew. This agony was to continue for several more minutes, for as each of Ryder's ships passed by, they added to the misery of those on board by riddling the guard ship with Oerlikon fire.

Prime target of the enemy fire was the *Campbeltown*, its size and obvious importance singled it out for particular attention. Shells of all calibres slammed into its superstructure and decks. Small fires broke out and spinning debris flew off in all directions. Below decks shells and bullets were penetrating into her vital compartments. The boiler and engine rooms took hits, as did almost every other part of the ship. On deck, lying behind the welded armour plates specially installed to give them some cover, the demolition parties of commandos sought refuge from the flying metal, waiting for the moment when the ship rammed the dock and they could get to their feet and fight back. Everywhere, casualties gradually began to mount.

On the open bridge of the *Campbeltown*, Commander Beattie felt that things were becoming too 'hot' for the men gathered there and ordered them all below to the covered wheel house. There was some protection here from smaller-calibre weapons for its sides and front were plated, except for a strip about a foot wide which gave some forward visibility. Through this slit Beattie now concentrated on guiding the destroyer to her target. He asked for full speed and planned to hit the outer caisson of the Normandie Dock at 20 knots. For the moment, though, he could not see a thing, blinded as he was by a searchlight beam coming from a position almost dead ahead. At his side the helmsman was shot dead. The quartermaster jumped forward to take the helm and he too fell

almost immediately. Tibbits, the demolition specialist now stepped forward to guide the ship.

Ahead of them, Beattie concentrated his gaze on the motor gun boat, waiting for the moment when it would sheer away to starboard and allow the destroyer a clear run at the lock gate. The forward gun took a direct hit from a large shell which killed the crew and those commandos around it. The explosion momentarily blinded Beattie, but when the smoke cleared he suddenly caught sight of the curved jetties of the South Entrance. With his position on the river positively fixed, he gave the helm orders that brought the speeding destroyer close by the Old Mole, bearing down on the lock gates just a few hundred yards away. Just in front of him MGB 314 veered away to the right. 'Stand by to Ram,' ordered Beattie and everybody in the wheel house braced themselves for the shock of collision. Ahead, looming out of the darkness, but lit with the flashes of guns and swept by searchlights, was the low dark strip of black steel that marked the entrance to the Normandie Dock. Suddenly *Campbeltown* hit the anti-torpedo net that protected the lock, but the rush of over 1,000 tons of warship tore through the steel mesh and the destroyer leapt forward unchecked. Seconds later, with a grinding low groan, the ship struck the centre of the massive steel caisson and shuddered to a halt. It was 01.34hrs; Campbeltown had reached her target just four minutes late.

THE ASSAULT

THE COMMANDOS ATTACK

Campbeltown had hit the gates of the dry dock at 20 knots and its forward compartments had crumpled back about 35 feet. The bows of the ship had reared up over the caisson, projecting to a point just beyond the structure. The warship was lodged on the gates in such a position that the four tons of explosive in her forward compartments rested right up against the wall of the caisson. The charge could not have been better placed if it had been carried there by hand. It was a perfect climax to a magnificent piece of seamanship.

By the time the flotilla had finally been identified by the enemy as being hostile, *Campbeltown* and the leading ships had been well into the Loire and past most of the heavier guns on the river banks. Not so those motor launches at the rear of the columns. Their passage up to the docks was through enemy defences that were thoroughly alert to the craft on the river. Over a dozen searchlights of different sizes illuminated the water in brilliant white light and the fast moving grey launches stood out in stark relief. It was inevitable that the boats would suffer the combined attention of all the guns.

Lt Curtis's MGB 314, carrying Ryder and Newman, and the two leading torpedo boats that had raced forward alongside the *Campbeltown*, Irwin's ML 270 and Boyd's ML 160, circled around in mid-river opposite the stranded destroyer giving supporting fire as her commandos leapt ashore. Close behind the leaders, the two columns of motor launches now came up towards their landing places. The starboard column was set to land her commandos at the Old Entrance.

The Old Entrance

The leading craft in this line was Lt Commander Stephens's ML 192 and she was hit by a large shell even before the *Campbeltown* had rammed the dock. The missile tore a large hole in the engine room, crippling her immediately. The boat was thrown out of control and she veered across the river to the left, through the port column of launches, and struck the high stone wall of the East Jetty. Other shells hit the ship and started fires on board and it was quickly realised by all who were left alive on board that she was doomed. Stephens gave orders to abandon ship, but the high walls of the jetty towering above the small craft made disembarkation impossible. The wounded were put into rafts as the ship began to drift downstream, others took to the water. All but five of the commandos on board were lost, along with four of the crew. Captain Michael Burn from ML 192's Assault Group escaped the disaster, however, and made his way ashore, determined to achieve his objectives.

The southern steps at the Old Entrance alongside which Lt Rodier brought ML 177 to land Troop Sergeant-Major Haines and his party. The submarine pens are in the background located on the opposite side of the Submarine Basin. In the centre of the picture are the lock gates to the Old Entrance successfully torpedoed by Lt Wynn in MTB 74. To the right of the photograph, the large concrete monolith is a post-raid submarine pen with lock gates at each end which provided an alternative entrance into the Submarine Basin. (Author)

This he did, making his way alone to the site of the flak towers that he and his men were meant to attack, only to find them empty.

The next craft in the starboard column was ML 262, commanded by Lt Burt, carrying the demolition party of Lt Woodcock, whose objective was to blow the bridge across the Old Entrance and the two adjacent locks. Lt Burt saw Stephens's boat veer across his line and was momentarily confused by the searchlights and by having to take avoiding action. He was opposite the Old Entrance before he realised it and overshot his mark, roaring ahead by a few hundred yards. Behind him, the next boat, Lt Beart's ML 267, also made the same mistake and overshot. Each craft then turned around and endeavoured to land at their appointed places.

Fourth in the starboard column was ML 268, commanded by Lt Tillie. He saw the two launches in front of him overshoot the Old Entrance and made the correct course for the landing place. As he turned towards the inlet from the centre of the river his ship was hit by sustained and accurate fire from close range. In moments the launch was a blazing inferno as the highly flammable petrol on board ignited. Seconds later she blew up, spreading burning fuel across the surface of the water, just behind the stricken *Campbeltown*. Lt Tillie survived with just under half of his crew, but all but two of the 18 commandos on board perished.

The fifth boat in the line, Lt Fenton's ML 156, was struck repeatedly well before she reached the dock area. A direct hit on the bridge

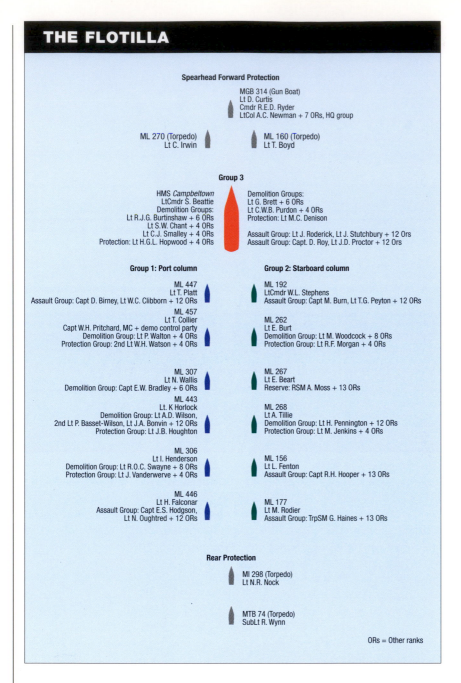

Spearhead Forward Protection

MGB 314 (Gun Boat)
Lt D. Curtis
Cmdr R.E.D. Ryder
LtCol A.C. Newman + 7 ORs, HQ group

ML 270 (Torpedo)
Lt C. Irwin

ML 160 (Torpedo)
Lt T. Boyd

Group 3

HMS *Campbeltown*
LtCmdr S. Beattie
Demolition Groups:
Lt R.J.G. Burtinshaw + 6 ORs
Lt S.W. Chant + 4 ORs
Lt C.J. Smalley + 4 ORs
Protection: Lt H.G.L. Hopwood + 4 ORs

Demolition Groups:
Lt G. Brett + 6 ORs
Lt C.W.B. Purdon + 4 ORs
Protection: Lt M.C. Denison

Assault Group: Lt J. Roderick, Lt J. Stutchbury + 12 Ors
Assault Group: Capt. D. Roy, Lt J.D. Proctor + 12 Ors

Group 1: Port column

ML 447
Lt T. Platt
Assault Group: Capt D. Birney, Lt W.C. Clibborn + 12 ORs

ML 457
Lt T. Collier
Capt W.H. Pritchard, MC + demo control party
Demolition Group: Lt P. Walton + 4 ORs
Protection Group: 2nd Lt W.H. Watson + 4 ORs

ML 307
Lt N. Wallis
Demolition Group: Capt E.W. Bradley + 6 ORs

ML 443
Lt. K Horlock
Demolition Group: Lt A.D. Wilson,
2nd Lt P. Basset-Wilson, Lt J.A. Bonvin + 12 ORs
Protection Group: Lt J.B. Houghton

ML 306
Lt I. Henderson
Demolition Group: Lt R.O.C. Swayne + 8 ORs
Protection Group: Lt J. Vanderwerve + 4 ORs

ML 446
Lt H. Falconar
Assault Group: Capt E.S. Hodgson,
Lt N. Oughtred + 12 ORs

Group 2: Starboard column

ML 192
LtCmdr W.L. Stephens
Assault Group: Capt M. Burn, Lt T.G. Peyton + 12 ORs

ML 262
Lt E. Burt
Demolition Group: Lt M. Woodcock + 8 ORs
Protection Group: Lt R.F. Morgan + 4 ORs

ML 267
Lt E. Beart
Reserve: RSM A. Moss + 13 ORs

ML 268
Lt A. Tillie
Demolition Group: Lt H. Pennington + 12 ORs
Protection Group: Lt M. Jenkins + 4 ORs

ML 156
Lt L. Fenton
Assault Group: Capt R.H. Hooper + 13 ORs

ML 177
Lt M. Rodier
Assault Group: TrpSM G. Haines + 13 ORs

Rear Protection

MI 298 (Torpedo)
Lt N.R. Nock

MTB 74 (Torpedo)
SubLt R. Wynn

ORs = Other ranks

wounded its commander and Captain Hooper of the commandos. Fenton remained in control and when the vessel was approaching the Old Entrance it too took evasive action and missed the target. Fenton brought the launch around in a wide circle and made once more for the Old Entrance. His wounds, however, were too severe and he collapsed, handing over the ship to SubLt Machin. Within seconds, he also fell victim to the enemy fire, as did the ship's steering gear and port engine. All three officers on the bridge were now badly wounded and incapable of continuing. With the craft in a poor way, down to one effective engine and relying on hand steering, its commander decided to withdraw downstream.

The pumping house alongside the Normandie Dock, the target of Lt Chant and his demolition team. (Author)

ML 177, last in the line, achieved some success. Lt Rodier came up towards the Old Entrance through all the devastation around him. Blazing vessels, pools of fire and screaming men marked the course into the dock area. Sustaining hits all the way up the river, Rodier held fast to his objective, slightly overshooting the entrance, but he quickly realised his mistake and turned his craft into the steps on the southern side of the Old Entrance just six minutes after *Campbeltown* had struck the caisson just opposite.

Troop Sergeant-Major Haines and his party of commandos leapt ashore as quickly as they could, anxious to have their feet on dry land at last. In perfect order, Haines took his troop into the labyrinth of sheds close by the entrance and made to join up with Captain Hooper and his team. Their objectives were to eliminate the guns on the shore between the Old Mole and the Old Entrance. But Hooper was not ashore, nor would he ever be, for he and his men had suffered the fate of many others aboard Fenton's ML 156 and were retreating back down the river.

The command boat MGB 314 now came off the river and into the Old Entrance. She had finished giving covering fire to the *Campbeltown* and was brought alongside the northern steps of the entrance to land LtCol Newman and his headquarters. Ryder used his loud hailer to order Rodier to bring his ML 177 across to the stern of *Campbeltown* and take off its crew and the wounded.

By this time the two launches that had overshot the entrance had come about to try once again to make a landing. First of these was Lt Burt's ML 262 who brought his craft into the Old Entrance and landed his troops on the northern quay. Lt Woodcock and his commandos, together with Lt Morgan and his protection party scrambled ashore from Burt's craft to do their work. At about this time, just a short distance away,

The pump room deep underground the King George V Dry Dock in Southampton. Lt Chant and his men practised over and over on these pumps, perfecting the skills needed to carry out their demolition tasks during the raid. The layout of this pump room differs from that in St Nazaire in being smaller and more confined. Note the long shafts which connect the pumps with the motors in the power room 40 feet above. (Joe Low)

the southern winding shed erupted with an enormous roar as the charges laid by Lt Smalley and his team exploded. To add to the noise and the turmoil heavy fire from a harbour defence vessel in the Submarine Basin opened up at close range on the vessels in the Old Entrance. The guns aboard ML 262 returned this fire as small shells and machine-gun fire burst amongst the crew and the scattered commandos. In the ensuing melee Burt cast off from the quay and began to reverse out. He had just cleared the steps when he saw Woodcock's team racing back towards him. Burt once again brought the launch alongside and the commandos all came aboard. Lt Morgan told him that the flare recalling all the troops for embarkation had been seen – in the confusion multi-coloured tracer had probably been the cause of this false sighting.

Burt again cast off and began manoeuvring into the open entrance only to see Lt Smalley's party running along the quay shouting to be taken off, their demolition task, the blowing of the southern winding shed, having been completed. Burt once again returned to the steps and picked them up. Finally, with a complete boat load of passengers, Lt Burt brought his craft around to make for the open water. ML 262 was then hit several times in quick succession, starting a fire on board and knocking out all of her weapons, killing Lt Smalley and many others in the process. Although damaged, her engines and steering were still responding and Burt opened up the power and headed downstream to make his escape.

Behind ML 262 into the Old Entrance was Beart's ML 267, carrying Regimental Sergeant-Major Moss's party, Newman's reserves. Beart now took his craft across to the southern side of the entrance and tried to set his troops down on the foreshore near the landing steps, but with little success. A few men got ashore but they were recalled almost at once when the small ship took a succession of hits and started to back away from the shore. The enemy fire was intense and concentrated, starting numerous fires on board. Flames spread through the vessel very quickly and within a short time the launch was completely ablaze, drifting helpless into the middle of the river. The order was given to abandon the vessel and those who could slipped onto rafts or tried to swim for shore. Moss and many of the others were killed by machine-gun fire whilst in the water, others burned to death or were drowned. Lt Beart and ten of his crew, together with eight commandos lost their lives.

Last craft into the Old Entrance was Lt Wynn's ungainly MTB 74. On its run up the river, the craft was hit in the engine room, putting one of his five power units out of action. Wynn now brought his MTB alongside Ryder in his MGB to receive orders. The position of *Campbeltown* sitting squarely on top of the southern caisson meant that he would no longer be needed for his primary task of torpedoing the Normandie lock, but Ryder might still require his torpedoes to be fired at the destroyer if it would not scuttle properly.

Campbeltown's commandos make their attack

Whilst launches in the starboard column were attempting to fight their way to landing places in the Old Entrance, there was much activity on and around the *Campbeltown*. After she came to her abrupt halt atop the dry dock gate, Beattie's primary task was completed. It now remained for him to ensure that his crew were evacuated and then to scuttle the ship

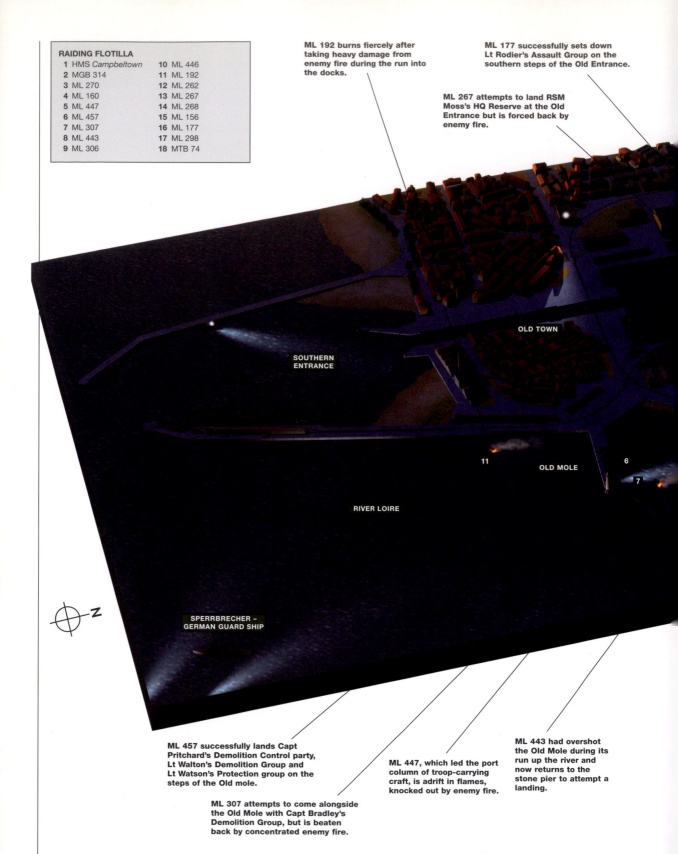

RAIDING FLOTILLA

1	HMS *Campbeltown*	10	ML 446
2	MGB 314	11	ML 192
3	ML 270	12	ML 262
4	ML 160	13	ML 267
5	ML 447	14	ML 268
6	ML 457	15	ML 156
7	ML 307	16	ML 177
8	ML 443	17	ML 298
9	ML 306	18	MTB 74

ML 192 burns fiercely after taking heavy damage from enemy fire during the run into the docks.

ML 177 successfully sets down Lt Rodier's Assault Group on the southern steps of the Old Entrance.

ML 267 attempts to land RSM Moss's HQ Reserve at the Old Entrance but is forced back by enemy fire.

OLD TOWN

SOUTHERN ENTRANCE

11   OLD MOLE   6

7

RIVER LOIRE

SPERRBRECHER – GERMAN GUARD SHIP

ML 457 successfully lands Capt Pritchard's Demolition Control party, Lt Walton's Demolition Group and Lt Watson's Protection group on the steps of the Old mole.

ML 307 attempts to come alongside the Old Mole with Capt Bradley's Demolition Group, but is beaten back by concentrated enemy fire.

ML 447, which led the port column of troop-carrying craft, is adrift in flames, knocked out by enemy fire.

ML 443 had overshot the Old Mole during its run up the river and now returns to the stone pier to attempt a landing.

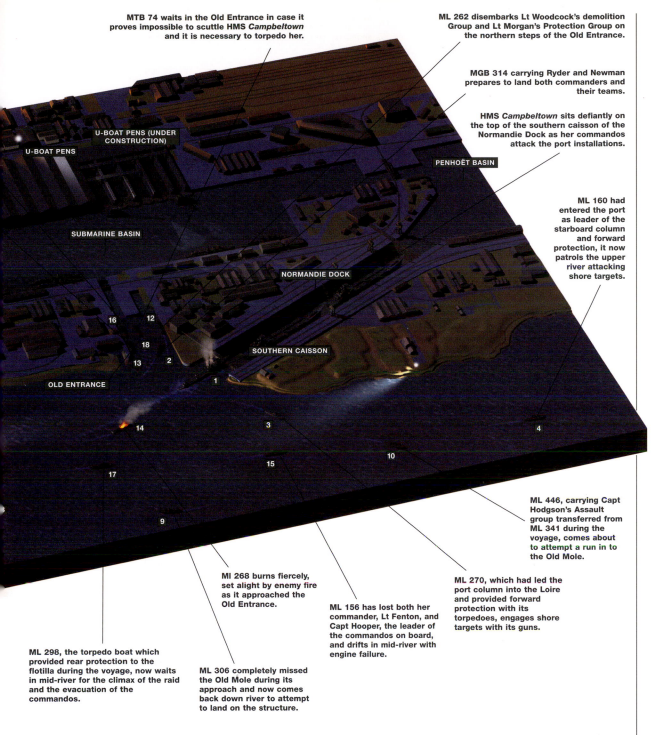

MTB 74 waits in the Old Entrance in case it proves impossible to scuttle HMS *Campbeltown* and it is necessary to torpedo her.

ML 262 disembarks Lt Woodcock's demolition Group and Lt Morgan's Protection Group on the northern steps of the Old Entrance.

MGB 314 carrying Ryder and Newman prepares to land both commanders and their teams.

HMS *Campbeltown* sits defiantly on the top of the southern caisson of the Normandie Dock as her commandos attack the port installations.

U-BOAT PENS (UNDER CONSTRUCTION)

U-BOAT PENS

PENHOËT BASIN

ML 160 had entered the port as leader of the starboard column and forward protection, it now patrols the upper river attacking shore targets.

SUBMARINE BASIN

NORMANDIE DOCK

16

12

18

2

13

SOUTHERN CAISSON

OLD ENTRANCE

1

14

3

4

15

10

17

9

ML 446, carrying Capt Hodgson's Assault group transferred from ML 341 during the voyage, comes about to attempt a run in to the Old Mole.

Ml 268 burns fiercely, set alight by enemy fire as it approached the Old Entrance.

ML 156 has lost both her commander, Lt Fenton, and Capt Hooper, the leader of the commandos on board, and drifts in mid-river with engine failure.

ML 270, which had led the port column into the Loire and provided forward protection with its torpedoes, engages shore targets with its guns.

ML 298, the torpedo boat which provided rear protection to the flotilla during the voyage, now waits in mid-river for the climax of the raid and the evacuation of the commandos.

ML 306 completely missed the Old Mole during its approach and now comes back down river to attempt to land on the structure.

ST NAZAIRE TEN MINUTES AFTER HMS *CAMPBELTOWN* RAMS THE DOCK GATES

28 March 1942, 01.45hrs, viewed from the west. HMS *Campbeltown* has rammed the southern caisson of the Normandie Dock and the flotilla of small ships are attempting to land their parties of commandos. The orderly station kept on the run up the River Loire has disintegrated into chaos as launch after launch is hit by enemy fire.

so that she rested securely on the mud of the Loire, blocking the entrance in the event that the charge in her bowels did not explode at the appropriate time.

The destroyer was now a stationary target at the mercy of the enemy guns, which continued to pound the ship. *Campbeltown* was hit repeatedly by great numbers of explosive shells, which penetrated her sides and caused a growing list of casualties amongst the commandos and crew. The German guns close by on the roofs of buildings poured down their fire onto the exposed decks. Across the river the 75mm gun batteries at Le Pointeau joined the barrage together with the quick-firing 40mm cannon on Minden Point.

When the *Campbeltown* had first struck, Newman's second in command, Major Bill Copland, began urging the commandos through the smoke of the burning fo'c'sle, over the sides of the ship and onto the steel caisson to set about their tasks. Lt Roderick and his team were quickly off the starboard side and made straight for their first objective, a sandbagged gun emplacement close by. The commandos stormed forward firing their Tommy-guns and Brens and were on the gun's detachment before they could react, knocking out the weapon along with its crew. The group then pushed on to the next target, a concrete bunker with a rapid-firing 37mm cannon on the roof. The gun and its crew were eliminated with carefully lobbed grenades and the troops inside the bunker shot dead as they tried to bolt. Then came the third gun, but this had already been destroyed by fire from the boats on the river. The final objective was the firing of the underground fuel tanks. These were reached and incendiaries dropped down their ventilator shafts, but the results were disappointing as the tanks refused to catch fire. Roderick had lost four men during the attack and it was now time to consolidate his position and put down a flank guard on the western side of the dry dock to prevent any German counter-attack into the lodgement area. The lieutenant positioned his men and waited, with one eye looking skywards for the welcome signal to withdraw.

The first team over the port side of the destroyer was Lt Roy's group from 2 Commando; its immediate task was to silence the two guns on top of the Pump House. The German crews had, however, decided to make their escape before Roy and his men got to grips with them, fleeing down an outside staircase just as the commandos arrived. Roy and his sergeant bounded up the stairway but found the guns abandoned. The two men quickly placed charges to destroy the weapons and retired down the steps.

Roy's next objective was his most important. He was to seize the Old Entrance bridge and hold it to allow the demolition teams around the Normandie Dock to retire across on their way to the Old Mole prior to embarkation. The bridge was then to be blown with the charges placed by Lt Woodcock, but, as we have seen, Woodcock and his party had come to grief on ML 262. Roy led his men through the narrow passage between the sheds towards the bridge and found it free of the enemy. He quickly set out his team to cover the approaches from all sides and remained there isolated from all that was going on around him, in the thick of the enemy fire.

Hard on the heels of Roy's party leaving the destroyer was the first of the demolition teams: Lt Chant and his four sergeants. Their task, probably the most important of all next to the elimination of the outer caisson, was the destruction of the pumping house and its machinery. Chant's task was to enter the pumping house and blow the great impeller pumps which emptied the dry dock. These were located 40 feet below the surface, level with the bottom of the dock. With these pumps destroyed, the Normandie Dock could be nothing more than a tidal quay even if the outer caisson remained undamaged. Their inaccessibility would mean that it would take months, probably a year to make the necessary repairs, denying dry dock facilities to the German Navy in general and the *Tirpitz* in particular.

Chant and one of his sergeants, Chamberlain, had been wounded in the legs during the run up the Loire and they moved with considerable difficulty. Nonetheless the lieutenant got his team off the *Campbeltown* and into the pumping house in smart order. They found the door of the building barred against them but managed to blow it with a carefully placed charge and went inside. Everything was just as they expected, set out in the same general pattern as in the docks at Southampton. The countless dry runs and rehearsals in England now paid dividends, the line of electric motors, the transformers, the panels of switch gear and the rows of meters were all familiar to them.

Sergeant Chamberlain was growing very weak, so Chant ordered him to stand guard in the motor room whilst the others went with him down into the basement which held the pumps. Chant too was beginning to feel the effects of his wound and needed help to descend the zigzagging staircases to the bottom of the building. The descent was fraught with danger as the four men felt their way down the metal steps into the darkness, each man loaded down with 60 pounds of explosives. The layout of the staircases differed slightly from Southampton, with landing platforms going off in all directions, confusing Chant and his men. They finally reached the bottom and the pale blue light of their torches illuminated a scene very similar to the pumping chamber in the King George V Dry Dock where they had trained.

Having practised the procedure so many times blindfolded, they set about placing and connecting the charges on the key points of the impeller pumps. Working silently in the semi-darkness of the subterranean chamber the line of four machines were wired for destruction. Each of the pumps was powered by a long steel shaft that descended from the electric motors 40 feet above them. The charges, specially shaped and covered in waterproofing material, were laid in positions previously decided by Pritchard to create the most damage. Working to a methodical pattern, each man wired his charges together and then joined them onto a 'ring main' of cordtex into one firing system. The instantaneous reacting cordtex was fired by duplicated detonators and short lengths of slow-burning safety fuse, operated by hand igniters. The great ring of explosives, detonators and fusing would ensure instantaneous detonation of all of the charges, whichever of the duplicated firing systems reacted first.

One by one the sergeants completed their work and called out to Chant that they were ready. With the explosives set, the lieutenant then ensured that the firing system was wired and primed. All that now remained was to ignite the 90-second fuse and withdraw. Although he was becoming weak from his wound and recognising that the long climb

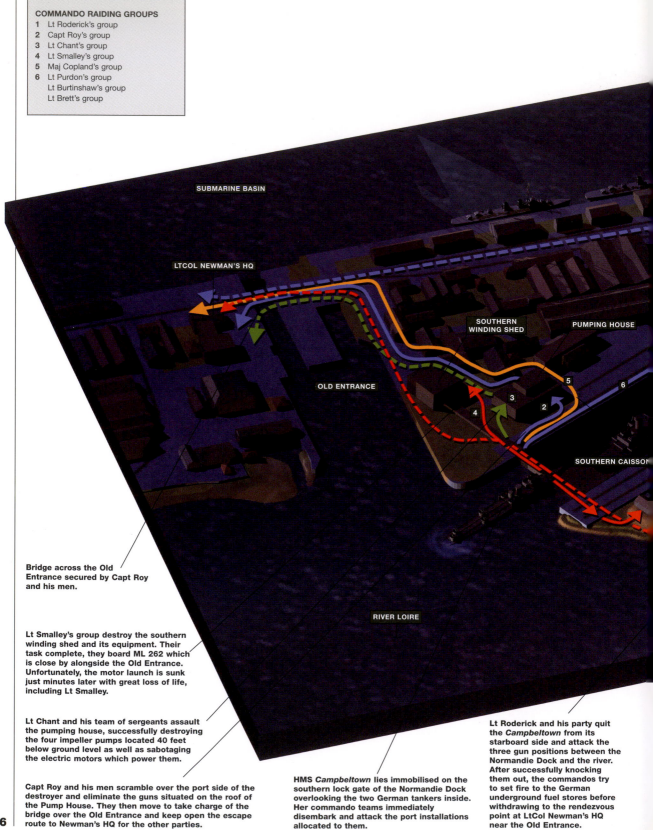

COMMANDO RAIDING GROUPS
1 Lt Roderick's group
2 Capt Roy's group
3 Lt Chant's group
4 Lt Smalley's group
5 Maj Copland's group
6 Lt Purdon's group
   Lt Burtinshaw's group
   Lt Brett's group

SUBMARINE BASIN

LTCOL NEWMAN'S HQ

SOUTHERN WINDING SHED

PUMPING HOUSE

OLD ENTRANCE

SOUTHERN CAISSON

RIVER LOIRE

Bridge across the Old Entrance secured by Capt Roy and his men.

Lt Smalley's group destroy the southern winding shed and its equipment. Their task complete, they board ML 262 which is close by alongside the Old Entrance. Unfortunately, the motor launch is sunk just minutes later with great loss of life, including Lt Smalley.

Lt Chant and his team of sergeants assault the pumping house, successfully destroying the four impeller pumps located 40 feet below ground level as well as sabotaging the electric motors which power them.

Capt Roy and his men scramble over the port side of the destroyer and eliminate the guns situated on the roof of the Pump House. They then move to take charge of the bridge over the Old Entrance and keep open the escape route to Newman's HQ for the other parties.

HMS Campbeltown lies immobilised on the southern lock gate of the Normandie Dock overlooking the two German tankers inside. Her commando teams immediately disembark and attack the port installations allocated to them.

Lt Roderick and his party quit the Campbeltown from its starboard side and attack the three gun positions between the Normandie Dock and the river. After successfully knocking them out, the commandos try to set fire to the German underground fuel stores before withdrawing to the rendezvous point at LtCol Newman's HQ near the Old Entrance.

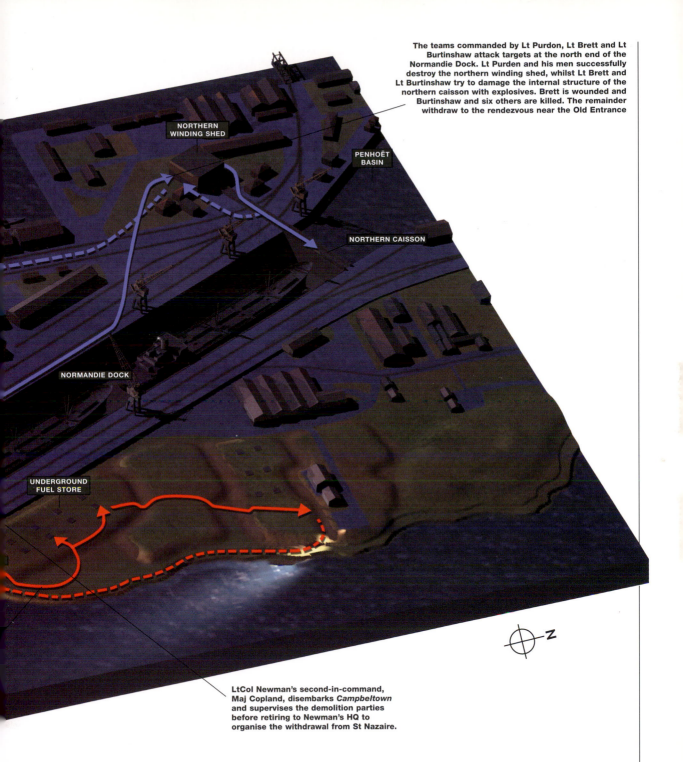

The teams commanded by Lt Purdon, Lt Brett and Lt Burtinshaw attack targets at the north end of the Normandie Dock. Lt Purden and his men successfully destroy the northern winding shed, whilst Lt Brett and Lt Burtinshaw try to damage the internal structure of the northern caisson with explosives. Brett is wounded and Burtinshaw and six others are killed. The remainder withdraw to the rendezvous near the Old Entrance

NORTHERN WINDING SHED

PENHOËT BASIN

NORTHERN CAISSON

NORMANDIE DOCK

UNDERGROUND FUEL STORE

LtCol Newman's second-in-command, Maj Copland, disembarks *Campbeltown* and supervises the demolition parties before retiring to Newman's HQ to organise the withdrawal from St Nazaire.

THE COMMANDOS ATTACK TARGETS AROUND THE NORMANDIE DOCK

28 March 1942, Immediately HMS *Campbeltown* rammed the southern caisson of the Normandie Dock, the commandos on board disembarked and attacked their targets. Many of the teams were under strength due to the casualties suffered during the run up the river, but all key objectives were attacked as planned.

to the surface would be difficult, Chant knew that it was his duty alone to control the firing of the fuses. He sent two of his sergeants, King and Butler, back up the stairs with orders to get Chamberlain out of the pumping house and in the clear, and kept Dockerill with him.

Chant waited in the darkness until he heard the shout from above that all was clear before he and Dockerill pulled the ignitors together. He watched until he was sure that the slow fuses were burning and then began the long ascent to the surface, aided by his sergeant, hopping from step to step. Once at the top they left the building as quickly as they could, taking cover a short distance away. Almost immediately the explosive charges rent the pumping house apart with a roar that was heard throughout the dockyard. The force of the 150lbs of explosive in such a confined space was devastating. When Chant and his team went back into the building to survey their handiwork, they found a scene of utter devastation. The greater part of the floor had collapsed and two of the electric motors had fallen down into the pumping chamber, with the other two twisted off their bases and useless. There was no need for any other demolition work to be done and so Chant's men contented themselves with igniting the oil which poured out of the transformers and set the place alight.

Outside the building Chant met with Captain Montgomery, who was in charge of the demolitions around the dry dock, and reported the completion of his tasks. With this done, he was free to withdraw to the Old Mole, through Roy's bridge, ready for evacuation.

Just before Chant's destruction of the pumping house, the night air had been filled with the roar of another great explosion when Lt Smalley's team set off their charges in the winding shed 50 yards from the *Campbeltown*. Smalley and his men had followed Chant over the side of the destroyer and ran alongside the water-filled channel from the caisson to the winding shed. Inside the building were the giant motors and wheels that wound the caisson in and out of position, across the entrance of the dock. The low single-storey structure was an easy target to attack and Smalley and his men were soon inside placing their explosives. Within a few short minutes the building was blown and Smalley reported his success to Montgomery. Job done, the commandos were given permission to withdraw. As we have seen, instead of making for the Old Mole for a controlled embarkation as planned, they took the opportunity to board Lt Burt's ML 262 which was close to the northern steps of the Old Entrance just a few yards away. Unfortunately, Smalley and some of them were soon killed when the launch took a succession of hits from enemy guns.

Following behind the men of Chant's and Smalley's teams off the *Campbeltown* were the groups destined to attack targets at the far end of the Normandie Dock. Lt Etches and his commandos were given the task of assaulting the northern caisson and its winding mechanism. Etches had two teams with which to carry out the tasks: first, to blow the northern winding shed and its machinery was Lt Purdon and four corporals, and, second, to attack the steel northern lock gate was Lt Brett and eight NCOs. To protect these men whilst they went about their business, Lt Denison and four well-armed commandos were to act as guard. To this group were added Lt Burtenshaw and his men, who were now available to assist because their main task, the blowing of the

The northern winding shed after Lt Purdon and his demolition team got to work on it. The remains of the great wheels providing the momentum to draw the caisson along its camber can be clearly seen in the centre of the photograph. The background to the picture is the Submarine Basin. (Bundesarchiv, 65/2314A/5A)

southern caisson should *Campbeltown* fail to ram the lock, was not now necessary; Beattie's expert seamanship had put Burtenshaw out of a job.

During the run in Etches was wounded several times in the legs and became almost incapable of movement. It was clear that he could no longer lead the teams to the northern end of the dock and so they left without him. Two of Denison's protection squad were also wounded in the legs and remained on board waiting to be evacuated, leaving just three men to guard the busy demolition teams. As soon as the *Campbeltown* had struck, Purdon, Brett and Burtenshaw were off the ship and making for their targets. The Normandie Dock is over 300 metres long and the small groups of commandos had to pick their way through the dark dockyard, keeping away from the light of the sweeping searchlights, dodging enemy fire.

Denison and his men led the way and soon came under fierce and accurate fire from a trench halfway along the dockside. In an expertly executed set piece attack, Denison diverted the fire of the Germans in the trench whilst his two remaining men hurled hand grenades. All inside were killed. Denison then passed beyond the northern caisson and winding shed and set out his small party to protect the demolition teams from any of the enemy who came across the northern Swing Bridge.

Lt Purdon followed up behind with his team and made for the winding shed, whilst Brett and Burtenshaw made for the roadway across the lock gate. Purdon's task mirrored that of Smalley at the other end of the dry dock. He and his men placed their charges on the motors and giant wheels and wired them up ready to be blown, but waited for Brett

59

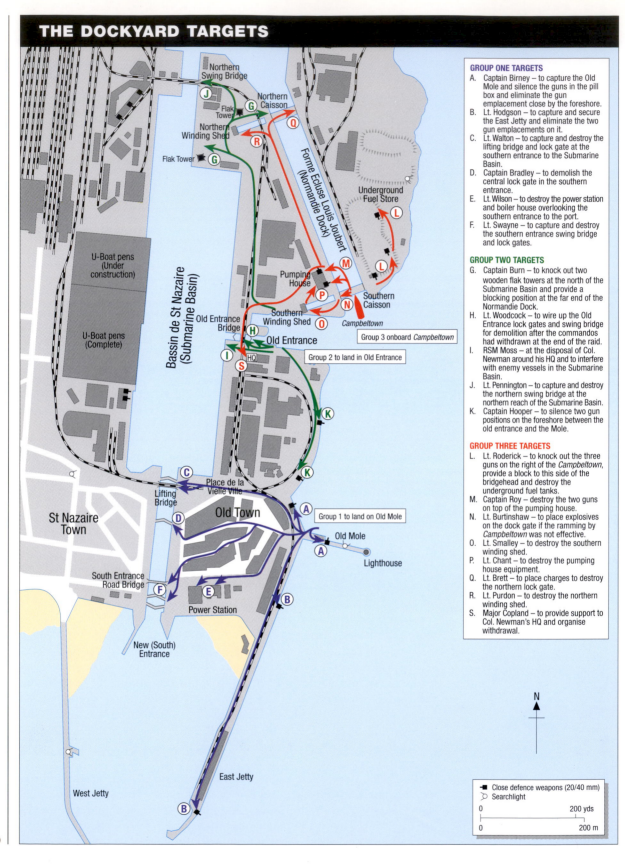

and Burtenshaw to blow the caisson first. Purdon sent Sergeant Chung across to tell the other two officers that he was ready, but the NCO ran into a fury of small arms fire and was wounded.

Things were very precarious at the northern rim of the dry dock. Brett and Burtenshaw were suffering unwelcome attention and a good deal of small arms fire from several groups of concealed enemy troops. Bullets ricocheted off of the road and ironwork of the lock gate. To add to their difficulties, the construction of the caisson differed from that at Southampton. The teams were to place two types of charge on the dock gates. One set consisted of 12 18lb underwater charges, which were to be placed against the caisson walls on the Penhoët Basin side of the gates, whilst the other set was made up of circular 'wreath'-like charges that were to be laid inside the hollow walls of the caisson itself. However, when the team tried to open an inspection door in the centre of the road to get into the chamber, they had difficulty because the top of the caisson had been decked over with timber and sealed with tarmac.

Brett was hit shortly after arriving and many others in the two parties had also become casualties. Enemy fire continued to sweep across the exposed roadway, picking off the commandos one by one. With great determination the underwater charges were lowered over the side and wired up into a cordtex ring main, ready for igniting. On the roadway, try as they might, it proved to be an impossible task to get into the caisson. Burtenshaw attempted to blow open the trap door, but failed; the sound of the explosion bringing even fiercer retaliatory fire from the enemy. Ships in the Penhoët Basin joined in the fire-fight, as did the machine-guns on the two tankers below them in the dry dock. German

Modern picture of the roadway over the northern caisson of the dry dock. Lt Burtinshaw's men were unable to get inside the hollow dock gate to plant explosives through the inspection covers seen in the middle of the road. The low square white building in the rear is the modern winding shed. (Author)

parties began to encroach on the exposed commandos and fire continued to come at them from all directions. Casualties continued to mount, with men falling on all sides, one of whom was Burtenshaw.

Both of the officers were now out of commission and it was left to Sergeant Carr to take control. It had become obvious that no charges could be laid inside the caisson, so he decided it was time to abandon that part of the demolition plan and to fire the underwater explosives. After ensuring that everybody was clear, Carr detonated the explosives, which were hanging from the dock gates in the water. They blew in a low and comforting boom which sent great pillars of water skywards. Carr returned to the roadway over the caisson and heard the reassuring sound of water cascading into the hollow structure. The dock gate might not have been destroyed, but it was damaged in such a way that it would take a good deal of time and effort to repair.

The task of damaging the northern caisson had been completed to the best of their ability and the injured Brett ordered the men to retire to the Old Mole. They left behind them the bodies of Burtenshaw and six others, all killed during the work on the caisson. Of those that made their escape, virtually every one carried some kind of wound. Word was now passed to Lt Purdon to blow his charges and demolish the winding shed. The resulting roar when the building went up cheered the hearts of the battered commandos as they made their precarious way back to Roy's bridge and the expected evacuation from the maelstrom of fire that seemed to be engulfing the dockyard.

Whilst the demolition teams who had landed from the *Campbeltown* had been engaged in their explosive tasks, LtCol Newman had come ashore from MGB 314 and began to organise his headquarters. It was located just to the south of Roy's bridge and by coincidence happened to be an existing German dockyard HQ. Newman had just seven men with him when he arrived at his location and the group soon came under fire from guns across the Submarine Basin. Sergeant Moss and his party were to have joined him as his headquarters troops, but there was no sign of the NCO or his men (Moss and eight of his group had perished in Beart's ML 267). However, shortly after setting up his headquarters, Newman was cheered by the arrival of Sergeant Haines and his men who had landed from Rodier's ML 177 and had moved against the expected gun emplacements on the shore between the Old Entrance and the Old Mole. In fact they found the gun sites empty and made their way to Newman's HQ to get fresh orders. Newman now deployed the group as a protection party and waited for news of the rest of his commandos.

The action and activities around the Normandie Dock and Old Entrance were just part of the raid now taking place. To the south around the Old Mole and the Old Town, simultaneous with the landings to the north, the launches of the port column of the raiding force were attempting to land the commandos of Group 1.

Group 1 land at the Old Mole

At the head of the port column was ML 447, commanded by Lt Platt. On board was Captain Birney and the 14 commandos who were ordered to assault the Old Mole and eliminate the two pill boxes positioned along its length. Like Stephens in ML 192 at the head of the starboard column, Platt's launch was hit by enemy fire with devastating effect as she

approached the Old Mole. The Oerlikons were knocked out with their crews and many of the commandos killed. Platt managed to bring the stricken boat close to the mole, but missed the landing place and was forced to reverse out and try again. From the stone walls towering above them came a storm of small arms fire and grenades. As Platt manoeuvred the tiny ship back towards his goal a large-calibre shell crashed into the vessel, penetrating to the engine room. In an instant the craft burst into flames and began to drift away from the stone pier. Platt gave orders to abandon ship and those who were able took to the water. Many were washed away and drowned, others died in the river; a few made it to shore. A little later help arrived when Boyd brought his ML 160 alongside to take off survivors.

Coming up close behind Platt's boat was Lt Collier in ML 457. He was more successful, able to put his craft right onto the landing steps of the Old Mole and set down his three teams of commandos straight onto the stone structure. The parties consisted of the demolition expert Captain Pritchard with his four-man control party, Lt Walton and his demolition squad and Lt Watson and his protection group. As the craft approached the Old Mole the commando officers had seen a group of Germans running along the stone wall with their hands up and thought that these were the troops manning the pill boxes surrendering. With the garrison on the Old Mole thus eliminated, they quickly got off the small craft and made their way ashore to complete their tasks. Collier reversed his craft away from the mole and took station in mid-river awaiting the recall to go in and take the commandos off again once the raid was over.

This aerial photograph was taken some months after the raid when Allied bombers had destroyed most of the Old Town and surrounding area. The southern road bridge across the New Entrance to the Submarine Basin has gone, but the lock gates and lifting bridge remain intact. The narrow streets and densely packed houses of the Old Town can be clearly seen in ruins in the mid-left of the picture. (Imperial War Museum, C3403)

Next in the column was ML 307 with Lt Wallis in command. The motor launch was carrying Captain Bradley's demolition party, intent on blowing the centre lock gate in the South Entrance. As Wallis brought his craft up towards the Old Mole he heard a warning cry from Platt. 'Don't go in.' Platt called, 'It's impossible to land.' Wallis, however, was too close to stop and misjudged the landing steps. High above the launch German defenders on the mole were dropping grenades onto the deck and firing light machine-guns. Wallis backed off to make another attempt but struck an underwater obstacle and grounded. German fire continued to rake the boat and casualties amongst the commandos rose to a point where Bradley decided he was unable to achieve his objective with the men he had. After speaking with Wallis the decision to abandon the landing was taken and the motor launch withdrew to the other side of the river where she engaged German guns and searchlights that were interfering with the raid.

Behind Wallis was ML 443, commanded by Lt Horlock. This craft overshot the Old Mole when its commander was dazzled by searchlights. Horlock took the boat around and attempted the landing again, but the chaos on the river and the strength of enemy fire forced him to withdraw. Lt Henderson, following behind in ML 306, suffered the same confusion and under the same weight of fire he too withdrew.

A German soldier with his submachine-gun keeps watch in a doorway as the net tightens on the British commandos in St Nazaire. (Bundesarchiv, 27/1488/2A)

Last in the port column was Lt Falconar's ML 446, promoted from spare craft to a commando-carrying vessel when the unfortunate Briault had to return to England during the sea passage because of engine failure. This boat, like the two others before it, also overshot the Old Mole. Both of its Oerlikons had been destroyed and their crews killed. The officer commanding the assault group on board, Lt Hodgson, was dead and two of his sergeants were wounded. In view of the heavy losses, Falconar decided that further attempts at landing were useless and withdrew.

Bringing up the rear of the flotilla with MTB 74 was Lt Bob Nock's ML 298, a torpedo launch with no commandos on board. Her role now was to wait offshore engaging enemy defences until it was time to evacuate the troops. Nock took his launch past the burning wrecks near the Old Mole and up beyond the Normandie Dock seeking targets of opportunity and German gun sites. His boat did not, however, escape the enemy's attention, suffering its share of hits and casualties just like the other launches.

Thus, of the six boats that were scheduled to berth at the Old Mole, only one had succeeded. Collier's craft had set down just 20 of the 70 commandos who were due to land, but these had immediately gone inland to set about their demolition tasks. Birney's team who were due to capture and hold the stone pier, had been destroyed on the river. The Old Mole was still safely in German hands and would now be impossible to capture with the forces available. Out on the river, several small craft were ablaze and the others were under concentrated enemy fire. The location and means of evacuation of the troops ashore were gradually being put beyond the reach of Newman and his men, but all this was unknown to the colonel, for at that moment he was receiving the welcoming news of the successful demolitions around the Normandie Dock. As far as Newman was concerned the operation was progressing remarkably well.

THE FIGHTING IN THE DOCKYARD

Just 15 minutes after the *Campbeltown* had struck, the situation on the river was chaotic: craft were sinking, boats were on fire and blazing pools of petrol had spread across the water. Wounded men were screaming for help, whilst others died silently, alone in their pain and suffering. The German fire from both banks had continued unabated since the raiding force had arrived, giving no respite whatsoever to the exposed craft. Time and again already stricken launches took more hits, steadily increasing the tally of wounded and disfiguring the dead. With no shelter to be had, and with few serviceable guns remaining with which to retaliate, all sane men on the river knew that the raid was over. Some of the motor launches began heading back down the Loire towards the open sea, their commanders realising that to stay in the deadly waters off St Nazaire meant inevitable destruction.

Just inland from the Old Mole, the only groups to land on that exposed stone wall were intent on achieving their objectives. The first ashore from Collier's launch was Lt Watson and his protection party. He mistakenly thought that Birney's team had landed and taken the mole

Taken on the morning of the raid, this picture shows German soldiers using a mobile 20mm cannon against a house opposite the waterfront. It was said that the stubborn lone commando inside refused all attempts to get him to surrender and was finally subdued by this quick-firing gun at around 07.00hrs. (Bundesarchiv 65/2301/26)

and so he moved off immediately with Walton's and Pritchard's parties in the rear, into the face of withering German fire.

Captain Pritchard's role was as demolition control. Having trained individual groups for their tasks, he was present to ensure a smooth operation. He therefore had no specific targets of his own. Lt Walton's team were earmarked to destroy the lifting bridge to help isolate the Old Town from the remainder of St Nazaire and prevent any German counter-attack from that quarter. Lt Watson and his four men were there to provide close protection whilst the others went about their work.

Watson and Walton quickly became separated when they approached Place de la Vielle Ville (Old Town Place). The open nature of this part of the town made it a very inhospitable spot; German small arms fire criss-crossed the area and kept all movement to a minimum. Watson and his men tried to move around the western side but ran into immediate trouble and were forced to take cover. Walton attempted to get to the other side of the square to make for the lifting bridge, but ran into a burst of enemy fire and was seen to fall; his team remained under cover, it being impossible to move. Several men were shot where they lay, Watson himself was injured. The enemy were all around, and bullets were slamming into the exposed commandos from all directions.

Captain Pritchard and his four-man team took another route to Bridge D, avoiding Old Town Place. When they arrived at the lifting bridge they found it deserted, but the area around the structure was very open with the only cover available being a square hut just to the left of the bridge. On the other side of the lock an enemy pill box kept up a

steady stream of fire. The five men crouched behind the hut and waited for Walton's party to arrive but no one came. Pritchard spotted two ships berthed a few yards away in the Submarine Basin and decided to attack them. With Corporal Maclagan alongside to help, he sprinted the 60 yards of open roadway to the quayside where the ships were tied up, they were the French tugs *Champion* and *Pornic*. The two men climbed on board the first vessel and lowered a charge between it and the ship alongside, pulled the igniter and dashed back to the shelter of the hut.

Pritchard then decided to take Maclagan with him to check on the progress of the other teams who were due to blow the southern bridge and the lock gates. He left orders for his remaining corporals to do what they could to the lifting bridge and set off to the south at the same moment that the charges he had just placed exploded with a stifled boom.

The two men moved quickly down the long lock that links the South Entrance to the Submarine Basin, expecting to come across the three demolition teams going about their work, but there was no sign of Captain Bradley, Lieutenants Wilson or Swayne, or indeed any of their men. Pritchard then tried the power station, but all was quiet there also. It quickly became clear that no other commandos had landed. Pritchard decided to return to the lifting bridge and the two men began to move silently through the narrow winding streets but had the misfortune to run into a lone German as they rounded a corner. Pritchard fell back immediately, blood streaming from a stomach wound. The Captain had been stabbed, probably by a bayonet. Maclagan stepped forward and riddled the startled German with his Tommy-gun. Pritchard, clearly in pain and dying, ordered his corporal to go back with the others.

Maclagan was loathe to leave his officer, but resolved to return with some help. When he arrived at the concrete hut by the bridge he found

The Old Mole at low tide. The pill boxes are gone but the remainder of the structure and the lighthouse appear as they were on the night of the raid. The steps alongside which Collier brought his motor launch to land his commandos can be seen in the centre of the picture. (Author)

it deserted, except for the body of Lt Walton, so he pressed on to Newman's HQ to seek help there. (After the battle, the enemy found charges had been placed on the bridge. Whether these had been planted by Walton in a lone attempt to blow his objective, or by Pritchard's corporals is not known.)

Back in Old Town Place, Watson had tried again to get to Bridge D, but once more ran into pockets of enemy resistance and was further separated from the other commandos. He decided to make for Newman's HQ to report on the precarious situation at the Old Mole.

THE RIVER BATTLE

On the other side of Newman's HQ, close by the Old Entrance, Commander Ryder inspected the *Campbeltown*. There was no longer anyone on board and the commander was pleased to hear the crump of the scuttling charges explode in the stern and saw the old destroyer start to settle on the bottom of the Loire. Commander Beattie and his men had completed their final task and now looked for carriage home.

With the *Campbeltown* well and truly stuck on the lock gates, there was no longer any need for Wynn's MTB 74 to be kept in hand. Ryder gave Lt Wynn the word for the craft to attack the outer lock gates of the Submarine Basin with his unique torpedoes. It was the moment Wynn had been waiting for. His vessel had been surplus to anyone's requirements for so long and now here, at last, was a task suitable for its special talents. With a great roar, the motor torpedo boat was turned

Lt Wynn's MTB 74 at speed. The two massive high-mounted torpedo tubes give the boat a powerful profile. Capable of almost 40 knots, it was easily the fastest craft on the raid. (Vosper Thornycroft)

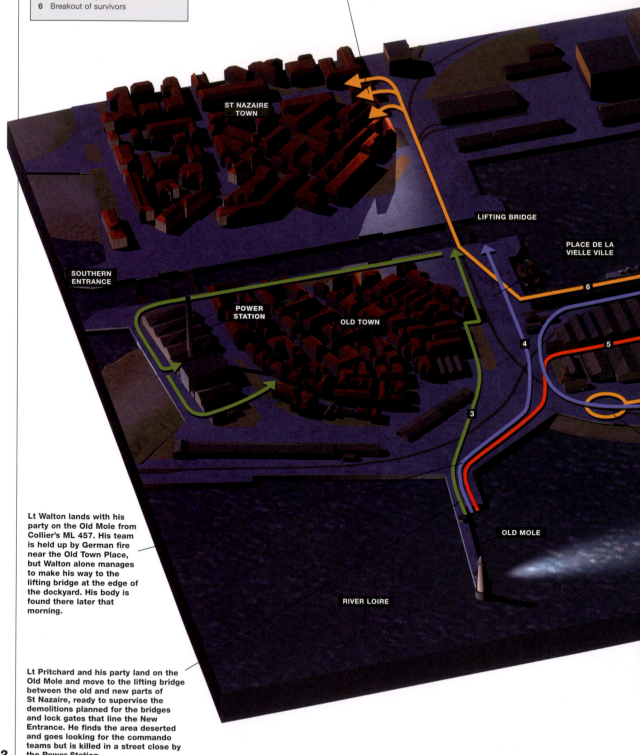

UNIT KEY

1 LtCol Newman's command group
2 RSM Haines group
3 Lt Pritchard's group
4 Lt Walton's group
5 Lt Watson's group
6 Breakout of survivors

Route taken by the survivors attempting to breakout from the docks. Once over the lifting bridge and into the built-up area of St Nazaire, the commandos dispersed into the back streets of the town, trying to make for the open countryside.

ST NAZAIRE TOWN

LIFTING BRIDGE

PLACE DE LA VIELLE VILLE

6

SOUTHERN ENTRANCE

POWER STATION

OLD TOWN

4

5

3

OLD MOLE

RIVER LOIRE

Lt Walton lands with his party on the Old Mole from Collier's ML 457. His team is held up by German fire near the Old Town Place, but Walton alone manages to make his way to the lifting bridge at the edge of the dockyard. His body is found there later that morning.

Lt Pritchard and his party land on the Old Mole and move to the lifting bridge between the old and new parts of St Nazaire, ready to supervise the demolitions planned for the bridges and lock gates that line the New Entrance. He finds the area deserted and goes looking for the commando teams but is killed in a street close by the Power Station.

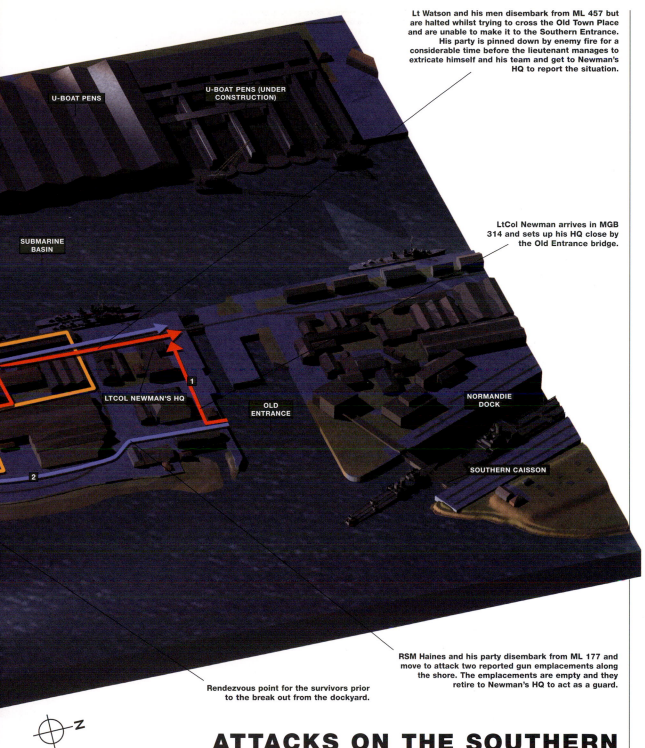

Lt Watson and his men disembark from ML 457 but are halted whilst trying to cross the Old Town Place and are unable to make it to the Southern Entrance. His party is pinned down by enemy fire for a considerable time before the lieutenant manages to extricate himself and his team and get to Newman's HQ to report the situation.

U-BOAT PENS

U-BOAT PENS (UNDER CONSTRUCTION)

LtCol Newman arrives in MGB 314 and sets up his HQ close by the Old Entrance bridge.

SUBMARINE BASIN

LTCOL NEWMAN'S HQ

OLD ENTRANCE

NORMANDIE DOCK

SOUTHERN CAISSON

RSM Haines and his party disembark from ML 177 and move to attack two reported gun emplacements along the shore. The emplacements are empty and they retire to Newman's HQ to act as a guard.

Rendezvous point for the survivors prior to the break out from the dockyard.

Z

ATTACKS ON THE SOUTHERN TARGETS AND THE BREAKOUT

28 March 1942, viewed from the west. The landings on the Old Mole are unsuccessful, with only ML 457 able to disembark its commandos. With the Mole in German hands and the motor launches having been destroyed or withdrawn, the commandos have no alternative but to attempt a breakout from the dock area.

around in a wide loop and ran at speed through the Old Entrance towards the closed lock. In a moment, the great missiles leapt from their tubes and crashed against the gates with a reassuring clang, sinking slowly to the bottom to await the moment when their time delay fuses would activate. His job completed Wynn returned to the rear of the *Campbeltown* to take off more of its redundant crew and wounded commandos, then made for the river and the open sea.

Wynn's boat, powered by its five engines, could reach 40 knots, easily enough headway to outrun the heavy German guns which lined the river expectantly, waiting for the British to make the return journey. At that speed the open sea was just ten minutes away. Wynn duly gave the order for full speed and the small craft instantly leapt forward, pushing a huge white bow wave before her. Five minutes into the journey, Wynn spotted two men on a Carley float drifting in mid-river. Standing orders were that no boat should stop to pick up survivors, but Wynn could not bring himself to roar past the unfortunate men on the float and he slowed his boat to a halt and brought it gently alongside the bobbing inflatable. With his vessel dead in the water Wynn had lost his one advantage over the enemy, to make matters worst, he had stopped right in front of Dieckemann's 170mm guns on Pointe de l'Eve. Almost immediately, the torpedo boat was hit by two large shells and set on fire. It was the end, Wynn gave the order to abandon the craft and those who could soon took to the water.

The three motor torpedo boats, ML 160, 270 and ML 298, that had protected the flotilla up the river, had been standing off the Old Entrance engaging German gun positions whilst the commandos landed. Irwin's ML 270 soon received a hit in the stern which severed her steering gear, rendering the boat useless until she was rigged for hand steering. Her erratic steering prohibited her from any further part in the action. With no commandos on board to be landed, Irwin brought the craft into the middle of the river and headed for home.

ML 160 with Lt Boyd in command was also hit several times soon after the *Campbeltown* had struck. With the situation chaotic both in the Old Entrance and around the Old Mole, Boyd took his craft to the aid of Platt's burning ML 447, just off the stone pier. He brought his launch alongside the flaming vessel and began taking off the wounded men. When everyone bar the dead were on board, Boyd made haste to leave the stricken vessel, as he was acutely aware of being illuminated by the glare of its flames. A short way downriver, Boyd stopped his boat once again to rescue three more men from the water. He was now within range of the larger guns on Pointe de l'Eve and a salvo from Dieckmann's artillery straddled the craft, causing more damage and more casualties. Luck was with him and he was soon under way again, albeit at a slow pace with only one engine working. Nonetheless he gained the open sea and his crew repaired the damaged engine to give him full power on his bid for home.

Lt Nock's ML 298 suffered the same battering by enemy guns as did the others. After taking hits whilst circling around in mid-river, Nock decided it was time for home. He approached both the Old Entrance and Mole looking for commandos to embark, but found none. A fire started astern when burning fuel in the water set the launch alight and the blaze became worse as Nock headed down river. The flaming craft

Bodies of those killed during the attack. The soldier in the background is German and the photographer has covered his face out of respect. The body in the foreground has been rolled over on his back and had his boots removed, suggesting that he was British, but why is he wearing a greatcoat for the raid? This would have restricted movement and covered his white webbing worn by all of the British as an aid to recognition in the dark. If he was German, why remove the boots?
(Bundesarchiv, 65/2313A/14)

acted as a beacon for the enemy guns ashore and the ship took several large-calibre hits when close to Les Morées Tower. Many of the crew by this time were dead or injured and Nock was forced to abandon the ship. The survivors taking to the water on the two Carley rafts.

Burt's ML 262 was moving downstream having picked up Lt Smalley's team when he came across Collier's ML 457 just off the Old Mole. Collier had made the only successful landing on the stone structure and was now in difficulties, drifting and on fire. Burt did not hesitate to go to his assistance and drew carefully alongside the burning vessel. Several German searchlights locked onto the stationary motor launches and hits from enemy guns followed in quick succession. The bridge, engine room and the area aft on Burt's launch all took hits from large shells which devastated the small ship. The order to abandon was given and those still alive went over the sides into the dark waters. There were few survivors.

Lt Rodier had successfully manoeuvred his ML 177 into the Old Entrance and landed his commandos, taken off many of the crew of the *Campbeltown* and was now making his way back down the river with some 50 men on board. He had completed his task as planned. Ahead of him, Lt Fenton in ML 156 was also making for the home, his craft limping along on one engine and steered by hand. Rodier's boat almost made it to the open sea before it was hit by 75mm shells from the guns on Le Pointeau and sunk. Rodier was killed along with Lt Tibbits, but Lt Commander Beattie survived in the water clinging to a piece of the wreckage until rescued by the enemy.

The commanders on the other launches out on the river had also concluded that there was no longer any chance of getting into a berth from which they could land their commandos or evacuate others. The four launches in the rear of the port column could not land on the Old

Mole, nor were they able to bring effective fire on enemy gun positions. One by one they turned away from the firestorm of St Nazaire. Wallis (ML307), Horlock (ML 443), Henderson (ML 306) and Falconar (ML 446) all took their motor launches back through the quick-firing cannon near the port, past the larger guns on Pointe de l'Eve, Pointe de Chémoulin, Le Pointeau and Pointe de St Gildas and into the open sea, making good their escape.

Still on his motor gun boat in the Old Entrance was Commander Ryder. He had seen the *Campbeltown* scuttled and watched Wynn torpedo the lock. He was very satisfied with the night's work so far. He then gave Curtis the order to take MGB 314 out into the river to see how things were shaping up around the Old Mole. The devastation that greeted Ryder out on the river filled him with dismay. All around were burning hulks and pools of liquid flame, the river seemed to be full of floating bodies and twisted wreckage. Very soon the boat was spotted by several enemy guns on both sides of the Loire and small shells began to slap into the craft and ricochet off the surface of the water. Ahead of him, the pill box on the Old Mole joined in and opened up with particularly accurate fire from close range. This target was quickly engaged by the already wounded Able Seaman Savage on the forward pom-pom, the only gun still left in action. Savage silenced the emplacement for a while, but it burst into life again soon after. Again Savage concentrated his fire on the pill box, sticking resolutely to his task even though his position was receiving a hail of bullets from numerous other enemy weapons. Finally the pom-pom and Savage fell silent, overcome by the enemy's firepower. For this act of valour and devotion to duty, in the face of overwhelming odds, Able Seaman W.A. Savage was awarded a posthumous Victoria Cross.

It was now clear to Commander Ryder that there was no longer any chance of completing the evacuation plan, nor was there any hope of survival if departure was delayed a moment longer. With extremely heavy heart, Ryder ordered Lt Curtis to take the gun boat downriver and make their escape to sea.

Able Seaman William Alfred Savage, VC, who won his high award for the valour he showed whilst acting as gunlayer on the forward pom-pom of MGB 314. Throughout the raid he remained at his post, completely exposed and under heavy fire, engaging enemy positions ashore with steady accuracy. He later died of his wounds. (Imperial War Museum, HU1918)

THE BREAKOUT

The situation at LtCol Newman's HQ became grim when the full realisation of what had happened on the river became known. Corporal Maclagan and Lt Watson brought more bad news when they reported that the Old Mole was still in enemy hands and that no other parties of commandos had landed. By then, Major Copland had returned with the demolition parties from around the Normandie Dock. The band of commandos assembling at the HQ was growing. Every officer from the demolition parties who reported to Newman was injured. Newman and

The body of a lone commando corporal lies dead, close to a group of German troops from 679th Infantry Regiment. The lack of any dockyard details in the background suggests the location may be just outside the port installations and the unfortunate commando may have lost his life during the escape. It appears that the railway truck in the background may be at the end of a line. This might suggest an alternative location of the area just to the east of the southern caisson, with the underground fuel storage behind the fence to the right. (Bundesarchiv, 65/2302/18A)

Copland held a small conference when it became clear that there was not going to be any waterborne evacuation. There were just two options open to them: flight or surrender.

Newman put it to his major: 'Shall we call it a day?' he asked. 'Certainly not Colonel,' replied Copland. 'We'll fight our way out.' Newman smiled, it was just the answer that he expected from his second in command and this offensive spirit was echoed by all the other men when the situation was explained to them.

It was decided that all the commandos should be assembled on some ground near the water's edge where they could receive their orders. They were then split up into groups of about 20. Each group was told to make its own way out of the docks, through the town and into open country, with the aim of making for Spain and on to Gibraltar.

The most direct route from the assembly area out of the dockyard was across the Old Town Place and then over Bridge D, but the open nature of the town square and the German fire that still zipped low across its cobblestone surface made this inadvisable. So when the groups began their move, they therefore doubled back towards Roy's bridge and then slipped sideways through the rows of sheds to the side of the Submarine Basin. This brought them under observation from German guns across the basin and more men fell casualties to the sporadic fire that opened up on them. Many of the wounded dropped out of the march, unable to keep up with the able bodied, even over this short distance. Each one of them knew that in their vulnerable state capture would be inevitable, whether it happened inside the docks or outside,

OPPOSITE, TOP
Two German naval troops help a wounded commando. The picture is looking towards the lifting bridge and the new part of St Nazaire town. To the left of the bridge is the square hut behind which Pritchard and his men sheltered and alongside which Lt Walton's body was found. (Bundesarchiv, MW 3719/14)

OPPOSITE, BOTTOM
Modern picture from the same viewpoint, with the lifting bridge and the hut alongside appearing unchanged after almost 60 years. (Author)

BELOW **The Germans begin to count the cost of the raid in human terms. This wounded soldier is helped by two naval troops, near the lifting bridge on the edge of the Old Town. In the right foreground, Lt Stuart Chant lies wounded on the ground alongside other commandos; in the left background, two French civilians return to their homes. (Bundesarchiv, 65/2302/23A)**

they knew they would never make it to Spain. Others crept into hiding places, hoping to move on when the fuss had died down.

At the southern end of the basin, the huts ran up to the roadway close by Old Town Place. Ahead of the commandos, 60 yards to their right, was the lifting bridge and the exit from the dockyard. Each man who wished to make his bid for freedom would have to chance his luck over the open ground, then across the bridge's exposed roadway. On the bridge and on the other side of the lock, parties of the enemy were waiting. Small arms fire from prone figures grouped around a pill box whistled through the air, whilst inside the concrete structure a well-protected machine-gun spat out a continuous stuttering challenge.

For a moment, the commandos halted, trying to summon the courage to make the mad dash. Sergeant Haines set up a Bren gun to cover the initial stages of the charge. Then Newman gave the call: 'Away you go lads.' And away they went.

The sudden rush of rubber-soled British troops appearing out of the night took the enemy by surprise. With Tommy-guns blazing from their hips, the commandos dashed across the open ground making straight for the enemy. It was too much for the Germans on the bridge, they scrambled to their feet and took flight. Those defenders on the far side were a little more ready and they began a barrage of fire that swept through the ranks of commandos. Some of the fire went high and wide as they tried to adjust their sights to the close-range targets. Some of the fire hit and British troops fell wounded or dead, but the majority pressed on with little hesitation. Bullets struck the road and ricocheted up amongst the iron girders of the bridge, sending sparks and debris flying. Then the leading men were across and running amongst the

enemy. Fear and panic spread through the Germans as the 40 or 50 determined commandos fired pistols and Tommy-guns into them at very close range. In seconds the charging troops were through the cordon and had quickly disappeared into the back streets of the town.

It was here that the groups began to lose contact with each other as each man sought his own way out. Things were very different in the town, for German reinforcements had arrived and regular troops from 679th Infantry Regiment, part of 333rd Division, began to take an iron grip of St Nazaire. Throughout the night, straggling parties of men were trapped by road blocks and patrols. One by one they were captured or shot trying to make a bid for freedom (It was later estimated that 75 per cent of all the commandos making the break had been wounded). Colonel Newman and about 15 others sheltered in a cellar to wait for nightfall. They were soon discovered, as were virtually all of the others who were scattered through the town, when the German's carried out a systematic sweep of the whole of St Nazaire. With the coming of daylight the raid was well and truly over.

PREVIOUS PAGES
The commandos begin their breakout from the dockyard. Throwing caution to the wind the survivors of the raid make their determined bid for freedom, firing as they go. The charge, straight at the enemy defenders who were covering the bridge, took just a few moments. On the left of the picture Capt Roy leads his CO, LtCol Newman, on the mad dash across the lifting bridge, throwing grenades as he goes. On the right, Newman's second in command, Maj Bill Copland, empties his Colt pistol through the embrasure of the German pill box covering the bridge. Most of the commandos were later captured in and around St Nazaire, but five managed to escape and trekked right across France and Spain to freedom in Gibraltar. (Howard Gerrard)

THE AFTERMATH

With the coming of daylight, the results of the visit by the British raiders to the St Nazaire dockyard could be clearly seen. The devastation that the small band of commandos had wreaked in the port was impressive in its scale. Fires were burning everywhere, buildings were destroyed, ships were sunk in the harbour and bodies littered every street and alleyway.

Enemy troops scoured berths and sheds looking for commandos. One by one the wounded British Tommies were winkled out of their hiding places and rounded up. The Germans were very nervous, seeming to see an armed commando at every turn, letting off bursts of fire at shadows and each other. Their nervousness was further strained by the presence of the French population in the town. Some of the locals thought that the raid could be the start of the Liberation and took it upon themselves to silently attack any vulnerable Germans they met in the docks.

On the river, the bodies of the dead floated downstream and were washed up all along the shores of the Loire; isolated survivors of the sunken launches clinging to Carley floats were pulled from the river, and into captivity, by crews of German boats.

The motor launches that had made good their escape continued on their course to rendezvous with the British destroyers *Tynedale* and *Atherstone*, waiting 25 miles out at sea to shepherd them home. Ryder in MGB 314 had joined up with Irwin's ML 270 on the way out and both craft reached the rendezvous point at around 04.30hrs, but they decided

Moments before she exploded HMS *Campbeltown* sits high on the southern caisson of the Normandie Dock. On striking the gate, the forward part of the ship has crumpled back to a point where the four tons of explosive she carries rests right against the caisson wall. The positioning of this charge was perfect; it could not have been better set if it had been placed there by hand. (Bundesarchiv, 65/2303/12A)

not to linger in the area and set a course for home. As night gave way to daylight, Ryder spotted the launches of Fenton (ML 156) and Falconar (ML 446). At almost the same moment *Tynedale* and *Atherstone* came into view; they had been diverted by the presence of enemy torpedo boats that were patrolling off St Nazaire and had engaged in a sharp action with them. By this time many of the wounded on board the small vessels were in a very bad way and needed proper medical treatment urgently. All of the people on board each craft were therefore transferred to the warships and the motor launches were abandoned.

Four other motor boats had escaped the river. ML 160 (Boyd), ML 307 (Wallis) and ML 443 (Horlock) all made their way to England independently. The other launch, ML 306, commanded by Lt Henderson, was unfortunate to run into the five German motor torpedo boats that had been dispatched to patrol off St Nazaire in response to the sighting made by U-593 the previous day.

ML 306 versus the Jaguar

Henderson was 45 miles out to sea when he saw the five German ships coming towards him through the darkness and stopped engines, hoping that they might slip by unobserved. The larger ships passed within 100 yards of the motor launch, but a lookout on the last enemy vessel in the line switched on his searchlight and caught ML 306 in its glare. Action stations was rung aboard the German warship and all five craft began to circle around the tiny British boat. Expecting the British to surrender immediately, the German opened up with just small arms. Henderson replied with everything that was serviceable – one Oerlikon two Brens and a twin Lewis gun. One of the German ships then tried to ram, but the agile motor launch swung sharp round at the last moment and received just a glancing blow. The enemy raked the launch with her short-range weapons and Henderson's men replied with what they could. The enemy opened up with a shell from its 4in. guns and the bridge of ML 306 was hit, killing Henderson and wounding the remainder of his officers. The scene aboard the small craft was one of complete devastation, bodies littered the decks. The German destroyer *Jaguar* then closed on the stricken launch, hailing them in broken English to surrender. The challenge brought a burst of fire in reply from Sergeant Durrant on the twin Lewis guns. Already badly wounded, this sapper from 1 Commando raked the German ship with bullets. Coming close alongside, Kapitänleutnant Paul on the *Jaguar* called once again for their surrender. Again he was answered by another burst of fire from Durrant which swept across the bridge of the German ship, splintering wood just inches from Captain Paul's face. Amazed by this reaction, Paul took his ship astern to resume the fight, but could not depress his guns enough to immediately engage the motor launch. As the German ship pulled away, its crew resumed their fire, concentrating on the defiant Lewis gunner. Durrant was hit repeatedly, shot through both arms, his legs, stomach, chest and head, he collapsed onto the deck, dying from horrific wounds.

The only conscious surviving officer, Lt Swayne, himself wounded, decided to call a halt to the action. Of the 28 people on board, 20 were dead or wounded. Swayne stood up and hailed the German captain, offering to surrender. Captain Paul was suspicious, expecting a

Sergeant Thomas Frank Durrant, VC, posthumously received the ultimate honour after his brave and stubborn fight 'against overwhelming odds' at the gun of ML 306 during its naval battle with the German destroyer *Jaguar*. Sergeant Durrant is buried at the war cemetery of Escoublac close to La Baule. (Imperial War Museum, HU2014)

resumption of the mad fight. 'You must not play any funny tricks,' he shouted. Swayne gave his word of honour they would not. So ended this remarkable naval battle.

Once on board, Captain Paul commended Swayne and the British crew on their gallant fight and offensive spirit, singling out Sergeant Durrant in particular for his bravery. A week later Paul met with LtCol Newman in a prison camp in Rennes and brought the naval action to his attention, suggesting that the colonel might wish to recommend the sergeant for a 'high award'. Thus it was that the army sergeant was awarded the Victoria Cross for his valour in a naval battle at the suggestion of a German Officer. An event unique in British military history.

The End of *Campbeltown*

Back in St Nazaire the *Campbeltown* herself remained stuck fast on the outer caisson, her bows pointing skywards and stern settled in the mud. On board that morning were swarms of German sightseers. The

first aboard were the naval troops and experts, checking the ship out technically, realising that the 'old tub' was an obsolete craft, completely expendable to the Royal Navy. They saw the ramming of the dock gates as an attempt to sabotage its operational life. It did not occur to them that the *Campbeltown* might be loaded with explosives, or if it did, they did not carry out a thorough search of her forward compartments to find them. Presumably, they thought that the concrete sections were there to add weight to the front of the ship whilst ramming. The Germans were slightly amused that the British should think that the massive dry dock caisson could be destroyed by ramming it with a light destroyer.

With the naval staff satisfied, the British ship became a draw for troops and other German personnel. Visiting admirals and generals went aboard, together with their French mistresses and other collaborators. By the middle of the morning hundreds of curious people had arrived to take a look over the British vessel. At 09.00hrs, the latest time she should have exploded, the *Campbeltown* was still intact, her battered sides lit by bright March sunshine. 10.00hrs came and went, then at around 10.35hrs the pencil fuses so carefully set by the now dead Lt Tibbits, fired the four tons of depth charges in her bowels. The resulting explosion was colossal, sending a great shudder through the town. The ancient destroyer was rent in two by the blast, the front end blown to pieces and the stern section lifted clear of the water. Beneath her the caisson on which she lay disintegrated, collapsing into the dry dock, swept forward by the incoming rush of sea water. The carcass of the destroyer followed it into the Normandie Dock, flinging aside the two German tankers there on their stocks.

Debris cascaded down across the town, windows were blown in, tiles ripped from roofs and sheds flattened. On board the ship, tens, if not hundreds, of Germans were blown to oblivion, their body parts festooning the cranes and masts around the dockyard. To the listening British survivors the shattering roar brought them great elation; their suffering had been rewarded. Operation Chariot had achieved its prime objective.

ABOVE, LEFT **A squad of smartly turned out regular troops from 333rd Division, with a flamethrower in the rear, moving forward through the narrow streets of the Old Town. The debris on the road suggests that the *Campbeltown* has already exploded, sending broken roof tiles crashing to the ground. The area is saturated with Germans, with other troops and naval personnel seen on the pavements and at the end of the street. (Bundesarchiv 27/1487/17A)**

ABOVE, RIGHT **The squad closes in on an enemy. Real or imagined we have no way of knowing. In the aftermath of the raid the German forces were in a state of high tension. (Bundesarchiv 27/1487/19A)**

The German squad is now in action in the Old Town. The enemy, if they existed, were almost certainly French and local. However it is just as likely that this is an example of the panic and nervousness that seems to have spread through the Germans in St Nazaire. The flamethrower has been in use and has left a blazing path towards its target. Other troops take cover whilst the 'enemy' is flushed out with grenades and small arms fire. The photos are sequential and capture a brief but poignant episode in the aftermath of the raid. (Bundesarchiv, 27/1487/27A, 27/1487/30A, 27/1488/13A and 27/1488/17A)

Everywhere in the dockyard there was destruction, whether caused by the demolitions and sabotage of the commandos, or from the blazing debris scattered by the exploding *Campbeltown*. (Bundesarchiv, 65/2303/23)

With the explosion a new wave of panic and paranoia swept the Germans in the town. They seemed to see enemies at every street corner, alarm spread through the dockyards with German troops firing on any sudden movements or suspicious behaviour, whether induced by innocent Frenchmen or fellow servicemen. Throughout the day reports of sabotage by the French and demolitions by hiding British troops poured into the German headquarters and hurried bands of frenzied soldiers were dispatched to investigate, often firing first and probing afterwards. Further explosions two days later when Wynn's delayed-action torpedoes blew up the outer lock gate to the Submarine Basin, reinforced the German view that the French were sabotaging the port and planning an uprising, thus triggering off another round of frenzied activity and retaliation.

Whilst the many went into captivity, it is heartening to relate that a few commandos actually made their way to freedom. Five men evaded the German drag net that was cast over St Nazaire and trudged their way south towards Spain and then on to England. Corporals Douglas, Howarth, Wheeler and Sims, together with Private Harding made their escape through the French countryside in three separate groups, with Howarth travelling on his own. Each were assisted with great bravery by individual Frenchmen and their families, often at risk of their lives. Douglas and Harding passed from one family to another until they were put on a train to Marseilles, where an escape organisation took care of them. Howarth was eventually befriended by a schoolteacher who personally took him as far as Bordeaux by train. He was later picked up by the Vichy police and spent eight months in jail before he escaped over the border into Spain. Wheeler and Sims walked most of the way,

OPPOSITE, TOP LEFT
The wounded Lt Stuart Chant waits for his German guards to take him away into captivity. On his left is Sergeant Dick Bradley, whilst on his right the kilted figure of Private T. McCormack endures the wounds that were to cause his death a few days later. (Bundesarchiv, 65/2302/32A)

OPPOSITE, BOTTOM LEFT
Captain Michael Burn and Private Paddy Bushe of 2 Commando are marched through the streets of St Nazaire by German naval troops. Burns and Bushe were found holed up in the engine room of a vessel in the harbour and were flushed out of their hiding place later on in the day. Burns is attempting to give the 'V' for victory sign with his outstretched fingers, knowing he was being photographed for German propaganda purposes. (Bundesarchiv, 65/2303/20A)

OPPOSITE, FAR RIGHT
A Charioteer survivor wrapped in a blanket emerges from the German Harbour Commander's HQ. Judging by the wet foot-prints that mark the floor around him, he is one of the many who were rescued from the water. (Bundesarchiv, 65/2313A/30)

meeting a series of sympathetic families along their route. At the bridge at Leugny over the River Creuse, two pretty young women diverted the German guard's attention whilst the commandos swam across the river into Vichy France. All of these five men rejoined their units in England and saw further action in the war.

With the raid over, it was time to count the cost. Of the 611 men who entered the Loire in the early hours of 28 March 1942, 169 were killed, the great majority of whom died in the river battles: 105 of them were naval losses, whilst 64 were commandos.

The raid brought a great number of awards for gallantry. Apart from the Victoria Crosses awarded to Savage and Durrant, this high award for valour was also awarded to Commanders Ryder and Beattie and to LtCol Newman. In addition, four Distinguished Service Orders, 17 Distinguished Service Crosses, 11 Military Crosses, four Conspicuous Gallantry Medals, five Distinguished Conduct Medals, 24 Distinguished Service Medals and 15 Military Medals were awarded, together with 51 men Mentioned in Dispatches.

After the raid aerial reconnaissance photographs taken of St Nazaire showed just how successful Operation Chariot had been. The Normandie Dock and its port installations were rendered completely useless to the Germans for the rest of the war. It was not until two years after the war ended, in 1947, that the great facility was finally repaired. The *Tirpitz* never did venture out into the Atlantic and was finally destroyed by the RAF in a Norwegian fjord.

THE BATTLEFIELD TODAY

Today St Nazaire is an important and thriving ship-building centre, producing the very best of cruise liners for the world market. A visitor to St Nazaire intent on walking the battlefield covered by the raid will not be disappointed. From the vantage point of a redundant gun position on the roof of the indestructible submarine pens, the ground over which the commandos fought is laid out almost like the model especially prepared for the planning of the operation.

Closer inspection is permitted, for the enlightened French authorities allow public access to the port itself. Certain areas are fenced off for security and public safety reasons, but even then it is possible to get to within a few metres of the rebuilt pumping house and the southern winding shed, with just a mesh fence separating you.

There are many vantage points from which to view the existing southern caisson to the Normandie Dock, sited exactly where the *Campbeltown* struck at 01.34 on 28 March 1942. One of the best is from just by the Old Mole, around which Commander Beattie brought the *Campbeltown* at ramming speed. The Old Mole remains relatively unchanged, still with its narrow steps up which Pritchard, Walton and Watson disembarked from Collier's launch. The pill boxes are gone, but the remainder of the stone pier is just as it was, its lighthouse still winking out a warning to waterborne traffic. The Old Entrance has been changed slightly by the post-raid building of a massive single German U-boat pen with its own lock gates, sited on the northern quay where Newman and Ryder disembarked from MGB 314. On the southern side can be seen the steps where Rodier landed Sergeant-Major Haines's party. Between is the bridge so carefully guarded by Captain Roy and his men.

At the north end of the dry dock, the caisson attacked by Brett's and Burtinshaw's teams carries a road across it and public access is allowed. It is possible to stand there and take in the enormity of the caisson itself and the size of the dry dock. If you are fortunate enough to visit when the dock is dry, then the huge scale of the facility will become clear. Just off to the west is the camber along which the caisson is wound back in order to open the dock, the vast gate pulled by the winding shed in the background, rebuilt on the site of the one destroyed by Purdon.

Perhaps the most evocative site of all is the lifting bridge at the entrance to the port. It distinctive latticed girder construction remains virtually as it was during the raid. On the Old Town side of the structure is the stone hut behind which Pritchard and his men took cover and alongside which Lt Walton's body was found. It was across this actual bridge that the mad dash to freedom was made by the gallant commandos early on the morning of the raid. The commandos called it the 'Bridge of Memories', and across it at each reunion at St Nazaire since the war, survivors of the raid proudly march.

OPPOSITE, TOP
An aerial photograph taken some months after the raid shows just how successful Operation Chariot was. The Normandie Dock has been sealed and work is in progress restoring the facility. In the middle of the picture, the stern half of the *Campbeltown* sits on the bottom, the forward section having blown to pieces. The two winding sheds have gone completely and the pumping house, although standing, contains just broken machinery. At the bottom of the picture, Lt Roderick's targets can been clearly seen, as can the mounds of earth covering the underground fuel dumps. (Imperial War Museum, C3398)

OPPOSITE, BOTTOM
This photograph was taken just after the raid with the Normandie Dock open to the tidal waters of the Loire. The annotated print highlights some of the successes of the attack, with the concrete dam on the left being built to replace the lock gate blown by Wynn's torpedoes. (Imperial War Museum, C2370)

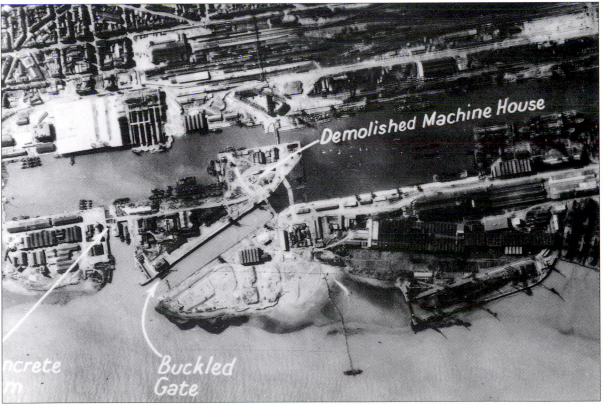

Demolished Machine House

ncrete
m

Buckled
Gate

ABOVE **The British Commonwealth War Graves cemetery at Escoublac. Here lie many of the fallen participants of Operation Chariot. It also contains graves of some of those troops lost in the sinking of the *Lancastria* off St Nazaire in 1940 and British airmen whose aircraft were shot down in the area. (Author)**

LEFT **The grave of Sergeant Durrant, VC, in Escoublac Cemetery near La Baule. Durrant's VC was the only one issued to an army recipient for a naval battle. Add to this the fact that the initial recommendation came from a German naval captain and the award is doubly unique. (Author)**

OPPOSITE, TOP **The observation post at the 170mm gun site on Pointe de l'Eve. The Germans made use of the French fire control post which was itself built on the site of a nineteenth-century coast defence fort. (Author)**

OPPOSITE, BOTTOM **The memorial to those who took part in Operation Chariot is situated just a few hundred yards along the sea front from the South Entrance to the docks. It lists all those who were killed during the raid. (Author)**

Out of town, along the shores of the mouth of the Loire, can be found pertinent reminders of the German fortifications and weapon sites that protected the port and from which the deadly storm of fire was aimed at the craft in the river. The determined adventurous rambler can locate overgrown gun sites and other intriguing concrete structures along the rugged coastline. And should you venture as far as La Baule, then take a detour a mile inland to the Commonwealth War Grave Cemetery at Escoublac and visit the graves of the fallen. Give them a moment of your time and honour their sacrifice.

There is one more important site to visit. On the beach front close by the South Entrance is the memorial to those who died. A simple granite plinth records the names of the fallen. Alongside is a tangible reminder of the ship that immolated itself on the dock gate, for just to the right of the memorial is the *Campbeltown*'s forward 12-pdr gun, standing sentinel over the memory of the dead.

BIBLIOGRAPHY

Chant-Sempill, Stuart, *St Nazaire Commando*, John Murray (London, 1985)

Dorrian, James G., *Storming St Nazaire*, Leo Cooper (London, 1998)

Dunning, James, *It Had To Be Tough*, Pentland Press (Durham, 2000)

Lucas Phillips, C.E., *The Greatest Raid Of All*, Heinemann (London, 1958)

Ross, Al, *Anatomy Of a Ship: The Destroyer Campbeltown*, Conway (London, 1990)

Ryder, Commander R.E.D., *The Attack On St Nazaire*, John Murray (London, 1947)

St George Saunders, Hilary, *The Green Beret*, Michael Joseph (London, 1949)

Scott, Lt Commander Peter, *The Battle Of The Narrow Seas*, Country Life (London, 1945)

Wingate, John, *Warship Profile No 5: HMS* Campbeltown, Profile Publications (1971)

INDEX

Figures in **bold** refer to illustrations